P9-BYM-167

ALSO BY JED POWER

DAN MARLOWE SERIES
THE BOSS OF HAMPTON BEACH
HAMPTON BEACH HOMICIDE
BLOOD ON HAMPTON BEACH
HONEYMOON HOTEL
MURDER ON THE ISLAND
THE HAMPTON BEACH TAPES

THE COMBAT ZONE

"Jed Power writes twisty, fast-moving novels that deliver the real hard-boiled goods. Check 'em out."

Bill Crider
Anthony Award winner
Edgar Award finalist
and the author of over 75 novels

"Good, tough stuff in the classic noir transition. More power to Jed Power!"

Bill Pronzini
Winner of the Mystery Writers of America
"Grand Master" award
multiple Shamus awards
and author of the *Nameless Detective* series

"The ghosts of hard-boiled legends such as John D. MacDonald . . . and—yes—Dan J. Marlowe himself haunt these pages. Pure pulp pleasure."

—Wallace Stroby
Author of *Shoot the Woman First*
and *Kings of Midnight*

"Author Jed Power has the . . . touch . . . it doesn't get much better . . ."

—Charlie Stella
Author of *Rough Riders*
and *Shakedown*

". . . Jed Power channels the tough-as-nails prose of Gold Medal greats Peter Rabe and Dan Marlowe."

—Shamus & Derringer
award-winning author
Dave Zeltserman

"Fans of Dennis Lehane will revel in the settings and atmosphere . . . an absorbing read . . . a hard-charging plot . . . Boston nitty-gritty."

—Charles Kelly
Author of *Gunshots In Another Room*
a biography of crime writer Dan Marlowe

Praise for *The Combat Zone*

"Power's work, already cover-to-cover forceful, keeps getting better. Boston has never had a better P. I."

—John Lutz
Edgar & Shamus award-winning
author of *Single White Female*
past president of Mystery Writers of America
& Private Eye Writers of America

Jed Power

Hampton Beach
HEIST

a Dan Marlowe/Hampton Beach Novel

Dark Jetty Publishing

Published by
Dark Jetty Publishing
4 Essex Center Drive #3906
Peabody, MA 01961

Hampton Beach Heist
Copyright © 2019 James Power
ALL RIGHTS RESERVED

Cover Artist:
Brandon Swann

This is a work of fiction. All characters and incidents in this book are fictional, and any resemblance to real people or incidents is purely coincidental. This book, or parts thereof, may not be reproduced in any form without permission.

ISBN 978-0-9971758-4-4

10 9 8 7 6 5 4 3 2 1

ACKNOWLEDGEMENTS

Again, I would like to thank my editor, Louisa Swann, for the excellent work she did on this novel, the seventh in the Dan Marlowe/Hampton Beach mystery series. I am also very grateful for the critiques of the manuscript along the way by my two friends, the superb writers—Amy Ray and Bonnar Spring.

Chapter 1

"HOW MUCH DID he steal?"

Dianne shook her head slowly. "I'm not sure. A gold ring. Couple of bracelets. A necklace."

We were standing in the bedroom of Dianne's Ocean Boulevard condominium. It was as feminine and attractive as my bedroom back home was a mess. I could smell her favorite perfume in the air. I watched as she pawed through the small jewelry drawers in a white dresser built into her closet. She'd called me earlier and told me she had a problem. That's how I ended up here at 9:30 in the morning.

"Are you sure it was all there?" I asked.

Dianne looked at me, rolled her green eyes. "Of course it was all there. Where else would it be? I don't have much jewelry."

"Okay, okay," I said. "I just wanted to make sure you didn't misplace any of it before we accuse him."

"I didn't *misplace* it. Do I look like an idiot?"

No, she didn't look like an idiot that was for sure. She was a smart businesswoman who was both my boss and my girl.

"When was the last time you saw any of it in there?" I nodded toward the drawer. It held tiny divided sections with earrings, rings, and other baubles in them. There were a few individual jewelry boxes located in a larger section.

Dianne spun around, stared hard at me. "How the hell would I know that? This is the 1990s, Dan, not the disco years. I don't wear jewelry all the time."

She was right. Except for a ring she wore constantly, her other jewelry was used only occasionally, as far as I could remember. Working as much as she did at the High Tide Restaurant and Saloon—in the back of the establishment, not out on the floor—there wasn't much sense in wearing good clothes, let alone bracelets and necklaces.

Dianne turned back to the drawer, resumed pawing about.

"Do you have an idea the last time you saw any of it?" I asked gently.

"I don't know, I . . ." She hesitated, half turned toward me. "That night we went to the Galley Hatch. When was that?"

I thought back as best as I could. Dianne and I had gone for dinner at the Galley Hatch on one of the few occasions we both were off from the Tide at the same time.

"A week or so ago, maybe," I offered.

"I wore my diamond earrings that night. Remember?"

I didn't. "Ahh, yeah. Has anyone else been in here since then?"

"No one." Hesitating, she added, "Except you."

"Well, if you're sure, it's got to be Sal then." I was talking about the painter who was currently our prime suspect.

Dianne's fingers frantically flipped over the little trays in the drawer. "The earrings. They're gone, too." She turned toward me, her eyes filling. "The ones you gave me, Dan."

Oh, boy. I put my arms around her, pulled her close. "Don't worry. We'll get it all back."

She pulled away from me, brushed some black strands from her forehead. "We won't get it back. He's probably already sold it."

"You've got insurance."

"Yeah, with a thousand-dollar deductible. But that's not the point."

"I know, I know. How much do you think it was all worth?"

She headed out of the bedroom. "I don't know. Except for the earrings, not much."

I followed her into the living room. If I hadn't known the elegant décor was Dianne's handiwork, I would have assumed she'd hired an interior decorator. The room had the pleasant aroma of scented candles. She'd gone over to the sliding glass doors and was looking out, her back to me.

"A thousand? Two thousand?" I asked.

She folded her arms in front of her chest and sighed. "Less than two, I guess."

I put my arm around her shoulders. Rain was battering against the glass doors. Below, on Ocean Boulevard, the traffic was light. The few cars passing by splashed water in their wake. Windshield wipers were on high. There was one lone jogger braving the rain on the far side of the boulevard. I recognized her. No other pedestrians.

Far out, beyond the sand, rolled an angry dark ocean that blended with the sky above it.

"How was Sal when he was here?"

"All right, I guess."

"Not high or anything?"

"No, he didn't seem high. I didn't see him that much. I let him in in the morning, and he locked the door when he left."

We were silent, but I knew Dianne had something else to say.

"Well . . . he didn't show up one day," she finally admitted.

"What do you mean, he didn't show up?" I asked stupidly.

She grabbed my arm, removed it from her shoulders. "He just didn't show up, Dan. That's all."

"Did he call?"

She shook her head hard. "No. He didn't call. I had to call him. He said he got busy with something else and couldn't make it."

That was a red flag, for sure. "Anything else?" I asked.

Dianne let out a deep sigh. Her shoulders dropped. "I called him at 8:30 the next morning to make sure he was coming."

"And?"

"He said he was on his way, but he didn't get here until eleven thirty. I had to have Ruthie go in for me at the Tide."

Ruthie was Dianne's good friend and a waitress at the Tide. She'd been there as long as I had, from the time when I was the owner. Before I'd lost the business because of my cocaine abuse. In addition to her waitress duties, she knew how to do most everything in the kitchen and behind the bar to boot.

"That's three hours," I said. I didn't hide the skepticism in my voice. "What did he say?"

Dianne frowned. "Traffic was bad."

Red flag number two. "He lives around the corner, off Ashworth somewhere, for god's sake."

"I know that."

I spoke gently. "How'd he look?"

"I don't know. I was in a hurry. I had to get to the restaurant." Again she hesitated.

"What?" I asked.

"It was just odd."

"What?"

"Well, just that when he was talking to me . . . telling me what he was going to do that day . . . he had his eyes closed."

"His eyes closed?"

"Yes, while he talked."

"Was he on the nod?" I asked, referring to a condition where someone's head lowers and they go into a dream state after taking a shot of heroin.

"No," she said. "I don't think so."

Then she added, "But they must have been closed for more than thirty seconds. I hadn't seen anything like that since I was in high school. I knew someone who had epilepsy and did that. But this was different. My friend in high school stopped talking when he had his small seizures. Sal went right along talking, only his eyes were closed. It was *weird*."

That was Red Flag number three. I decided to go for a home run. "Did he hassle you about money at all?"

"A little bit. He was hurting, that's for sure." She gave me a sharp look. "But we both knew that."

We did. Sal Mariani had been in the Tide many times, and we knew his financial situation seemed to be on a taut string just like lots of hard-luck beach people. But we'd never heard anything bad about him. Sal had seemed okay, and Dianne liked to help locals, so he'd gotten the job.

It's just going to be a triple, I thought, until Dianne suddenly added, "He did need a little money every day."

Not surprising. Still, I sensed something else was coming. "What?" I asked.

"One day he called me at work and asked for two hundred dollars. Said he needed tires for his car and . . ." She looked at me, expecting a reaction.

I shrugged. "So what? We both knew he was living hand-to-mouth." I urged her to continue with a roll of my hand.

"I wrote him a check; told him he could pick it up at the restaurant. When he came in, I tried to give him the check but he said he couldn't cash it at his bank. I told him to cash it at my bank. He said he couldn't cash checks at any banks around here. Told me some story about his ex-girlfriend overdrawing her accounts at area banks and his name being blackballed because he'd tried to help her. He wanted to know if I could give him cash."

Red Flag number four. A home run. "I don't believe that story. What'd you do?"

"I gave him two hundred cash out of the register. I felt bad for him."

"Do you owe him anything?"

"No," she said, "we were even. Except for what he stole from me. And that's gone forever."

"No, it isn't," I said. "Give me his phone number."

"Shouldn't we call the police?"

"You want the stuff back, right?"

Dianne nodded.

"Let me talk to him first."

Dianne headed into the other bedroom, the one she used as an office. When she returned, she handed me a piece of paper with a phone number on it.

"Do you have his address?" I asked.

"No."

"I can find that out. And don't worry, I'll get it all back."
I wrapped my arms around her, pulled her close, kissed her
hard on those lush lips. I forgot why I was there.

After a few seconds, Dianne pushed me away. "Dan, not
now. Jesus Christ. I have to get to work."

I stared at her green eyes and the face they were made for
and sighed. "Yeah, I guess I do, too." I reluctantly stepped
back a pace.

"Okay, I'll see you soon," she said as she turned and
headed for her bedroom.

"Remember, don't call the cops yet," I called after her.
"Let me see what I can do first."

I let myself out, ran down one flight, out the door and
halfway across Ocean Boulevard, to the parking area between the north and southbound lanes, getting soaked along
the way. I jumped into my little green Chevette and headed
for the High Tide, thinking about Dianne's jewelry all the
way and hoping that I could get it back.

I finally convinced myself that this problem wasn't much.
Not really. I felt good by the time my drive ended, except for
one little thought gnawing at my brain—that I seemed to
have a knack for getting involved in small little incidents that
turned into more. A lot more.

But that was just my imagination running away with itself.
Wasn't it?

Chapter 2

"YOU'LL NEVER GET him that way, Danny," Shamrock said.

I'd been at the High Tide for more than half an hour since leaving Dianne's. I stood behind the bar, holding the telephone receiver up to my ear. All I heard was the same thing I'd heard on the other two calls I'd made—an endless ringing. I hung the phone back up, thinking that Shamrock was probably right. This wasn't the way to get in touch with Sal Mariani, the painter.

"Maybe he's working," I said.

"Ahh, you're very naive, lad," Shamrock said from his usual perch, a stool at the L-shape end of the long mahogany bar. He had a Boston Herald spread out in front of him and a Marlboro cigarette stuck between nicotine-stained fingers. He wore restaurant whites, his usual garb in and out of work. He had red hair, freckles, and the map of Ireland on his face.

I shrugged my shoulders as I moved swiftly down the empty bar, laying out setups of ashtrays, salt, pepper, and ketchup.

"He's a painter," I said. "He *could* be working."

Shamrock grinned and shook his head slowly as if he were dealing with a child. "No, no, no, Danny. The eejit's a freakin' junkie. He's on a toot right now, for sure."

He took a puff from his butt, let the smoke out, and waved it away with his hand. "You said yesterday was his last day working at Dianne's. You can bet that's when he took the swag and got his dope. He won't be answering the telephone for quite a while. Especially if he thinks Dianne might have spotted the theft."

Shamrock was probably right.

"Let's go down where he lives and get Dianne's stuff back," Shamrock said.

"I don't know where he lives," I admitted. "Dianne doesn't either. Off Ashworth somewhere."

"Hmm," Shamrock said. "I haven't seen him down there."

Just then there was a loud pounding on the big wooden front door. I raced around the bar, unlocked the door, swung it open. I held it for the two men who came at this time every day—Eli and Paulie, my two first-of-the-day regulars. Eli grunted as he came in and headed directly for his usual seat in the center of the bar facing the beer spigots. He was a small man wearing a stained white painter's hat, shirt and pants. He had the ever-present Camel smoke dangling from his thin lips.

Close behind him was Paulie, his blue post office shirt the only hint of his profession.

"Hey, Dan," Paulie said. His brownish gray hair hung down to his shoulders in a style twenty years out of date. He headed for the L-shaped end of the bar and took a stool beside Shamrock.

I walked back around the bar, gave the two their usual beers—a draft Bud for Eli and a bottle of Lite, no glass, for Paulie. They both babied their drinks. I knew they wouldn't speak much until after the first one. That's how it was every day. Nothing ever changed. Not much, at least. And not often.

Shamrock acknowledged Paulie when he sat beside him but said nothing to Eli. A lot of people didn't go out of their way to speak to Eli. Let's just say he was often moody and could be very opinionated.

I leaned my butt against the back bar and glanced up at one of the two overhead TVs which were planted on the wall near each end of the bar. There was a game show on.

That's when Shamrock picked up our conversation again. "We got to find out where this stray dog lives, Danny."

I glanced at Shamrock and frowned. I didn't want to discuss this in front of Paulie and Eli. Paulie was okay, I guess, but Eli was as nosy as an IRS agent working on commission.

Sure enough, my warning was too late. Eli spoke. His voice sounded like his throat was lined with sand from the beach. "Where's who live?"

Paulie signaled for another beer. I got that and another for Eli, too.

"Ahh, no one," Shamrock said. Both of us knew that wouldn't end the questioning. Not with Eli.

Eli shifted his scrawny body on the stool. "What? Ain't we friends here?"

He looked from Paulie and Shamrock at one end of the bar back to me standing in front of him. When no one responded, he added, "And all the money I spend here? And none a you trust me? I'll have you know that these lips are pretty tight when they have to be."

I didn't call him on the fib, but I knew Eli, and I knew he'd be talking about this affront to his integrity for the rest of the day. I looked at Shamrock, rolled my eyes, shrugged, and said, "Maybe we should."

Shamrock waved his cigarette above his head. "He might know something. He's a painter too, ain't he?"

Paulie chuckled. "Used to be."

Eli harrumphed. "Whaddaya mean, used to be? I'm as good as I ever was."

Paulie chuckled again. "But you haven't had a job in years, for Chrissake. Just wear the dumb old uniform."

Eli nodded rapidly. "Well, I am gettin' up there a bit. Only take the best jobs now. I got the skill, and I'm in demand."

"When was the last time you used a paintbrush?" Paulie asked. He was grinning. I knew he didn't expect an answer and he didn't get one.

Eli scowled. "Never mind that. I wouldn't wear my uniform every day if I wasn't still involved in my profession."

"You sure it's okay, Danny?" Shamrock asked.

Through the big picture window behind Shamrock, I could see the Ocean Boulevard traffic building. No surprise there—the sky had cleared and the sun was out. Summer on the New Hampshire seacoast.

I raised my eyebrows. "You might as well tell him now."

If he didn't find out what was going on, I knew Eli would browbeat me right up until his drinking shift was over and he left. I couldn't take a few hours like that. Not today.

"Do you know a painter named Sal?" Shamrock asked Eli.

"Mariani?" Eli asked.

Shamrock and I both nodded.

Eli sputtered. "Do I know him? Is grass green? I worked with that fool kid. We used to call him Sal the Crapper."

"You did?" I said.

"Yes, we did," Eli answered. He stubbed out his smoke in the ashtray, one time for each word. "He'd spend more time on the toilet than painting. Finally we figured out what he was doing in there all the time and I hadda shit-can him."

"Whaddaya mean, *you* shit-canned him?" Paulie said. "You never told me you owned your own company."

"Well, *I* didn't really fire him." Eli's face turned a light shade of red. "The boss done that."

He shook his shoulders, straightened his scrawny body. "But I recommended it. Don't mind a bit a drinkin' as long as a man is careful and can handle it. Those ladders, you know. Ya can take an awful fall. I remember one time I was on a—"

I interrupted Eli. I had to; otherwise, we'd be in for an hour-long verbal tour of his painting career. "What about Sal? You know where he lives?"

"Ha," Eli said. "Of course, I do. We had to pick up the no-good drug addict every day to take him to the job site. That's when I was workin' full time. He didn't even have a car."

Paulie guffawed. "You don't have a car either."

Eli looked indignant. "Yeah, but that's my choice. Not 'cuz my money all goes for dope. I just don't like drivin' at night. So it ain't worth havin' one. That's all."

"Hmm, sure," Paulie responded. "It isn't worth it because I give you a ride back and forth every day. And it's not dark out either."

Eli furrowed his brow, looked daggers at Paulie. "Well, seein' you go by my place anyway, I always figured you wouldn't mind givin' me a ride. Now that I know I been a burden on ya, I'll walk, thank you."

"Never mind, never mind," Paulie said. "I'm just giving you the business."

"Well," Eli began, a scowl on his whiskered face. "I don't want you to have to—"

I interrupted again. "Where does he live?"

"Why you want to know?" Eli said. His eyebrows merged into one line and he looked at me hard.

I knew Eli very well and I knew that he wasn't trying to protect Sal the Crapper. He was more likely trying to leverage the information he had to find out what Shamrock and I had been discussing before he and Paulie had joined us. I was just about to make some vague statement that would get me out of answering that question when Shamrock interjected.

"He stole a big bag of jewels from Dianne."

"A big bag a jewels?" Eli said, a little life coming into his eyes. "No big surprise there. We had the same problem with him. A damn thief! One time he—"

"Where does he live, Eli?" I asked.

"What are ya gonna do to him?" Eli shrugged, held up his palms. "He won't give ya the loot back. He's a damn drug addict, for Chrissake."

"He'll give it back, or I'll smash his head in," Shamrock said loudly. He shook his big fist.

"No one's going to hurt him, Eli," I said as I gave Shamrock a disapproving glance.

"How'd Dianne get mixed up with him?" Eli asked. "You shoulda asked me first. I woulda set ya straight."

Dianne usually did her due diligence as far as checking on various contractors' histories. This time, her soft heart had gotten in the way.

"Where does he live, Eli?" I said in a serious tone.

Eli shrugged, told us where Sal lived.

"Hey, that *is* down near me," Shamrock said.

Shamrock lived off Ashworth Avenue, which was the back road on Hampton Beach that ran parallel to Ocean Boulevard. The street Eli had named was also off Ashworth, a few streets from Shamrock's abode, in one of the more rundown areas.

"Does he live alone?" I asked Eli. "Married?"

"Who'd marry him?" Eli said incredulously. "Got a girl-friend though."

The front door opened, and some local workers trudged in. They took their seats along the bar. Then came some timid tourists—first-timers—headed for the restaurant. One of our waitresses spoke to them and led them into the main dining room which was separated from the bar by a shoul-der-high, paneled partition that ran almost the length of the room. On top of the partition sat a long aquarium gener-ously populated by an assortment of brightly colored fish.

We wouldn't get any more talking done now that the lunch crowd was coming in. Shamrock rose from his stool. I hurried down to his end of the bar, motioned for him to come closer, away from Paulie and his ears. We leaned over the bar toward each other.

"Want to take a walk down to Sal's with me later?" I whispered. "Talk to this painter?"

"Is the pope Catholic, Danny? Of course I do." He scrunched up his red eyebrows. "And I'll beat the snot out of him, too, if he don't cough up Dianne's jewels."

Shamrock had a good heart and he rarely resorted to vio-lence but whenever a friend was wronged, he could get fiery. That's the way he was.

"No, we're not going to go down and make a bad situation worse. Just talk to him and give him a chance to return the stuff. If he doesn't, we'll tell him we're going to the cops."

Shamrock looked doubtful, but he said, "All right, Danny. Just tell me when."

"After I get out at five?"

"Stop by the house and get me."

"Will do."

Shamrock nodded and headed for the kitchen to do a couple more hours on the dishwasher before his day was done.

I turned back to my new customers. They hadn't liked waiting even the couple of minutes I'd just spent whispering with Shamrock. I didn't blame them, but I'd had to do it. Shamrock was a good man, and even though I didn't expect any trouble with this thieving painter, it would be good to have a friend along for backup.

I had work to do. With a little luck we'd have Dianne's property back by tomorrow. And if we didn't, the police would be handling the theft.

Chapter 3

AS SOON AS my shift finished at 5:00, I walked to Shamrock's small cottage, met up with him and we walked the few streets to Sal's house. We both stood quietly looking at something you might very generously call a "cottage." In the old days, folks around here would've called it a "camp." More appropriate would be the word "dump." And that was putting it mildly.

Sal lived at the end of a dead-end street, in an old one-story place that looked like it had been given up on a long time ago. Asphalt shingles, many chipped and some missing, formed the shell of the structure. The shingles were dark; either originally or they had started out lighter and had dirtied with age. The front yard, what there was of it, was no more than thirty feet wide and five feet from street to rickety stairs leading to a porch that could have been used as a set on "The Beverly Hillbillies."

In a dirt driveway beside the home was an old pickup truck, dull industrial gray with paint splotches decorating the body as if more than one can of paint in the bed had vomited its contents while coming or going from a job. A couple of ladders and paint cans were the only cargo I could see from this angle. Behind it was a car that I couldn't get a good look at.

The truck's presence told me our quarry was most likely at home.

I started for the treacherous-looking stairs. Shamrock fell in behind me. We passed two rusted rubbish barrels full of empty beer bottles and other trash. Flies buzzed around and there was a sour smell in the air.

The porch itself looked like it belonged to a hoarder who was just learning the trade. There were a couple of white plastic chairs and a matching table, all so beat-up I couldn't tell if they were waiting for rubbish day or if they were for practical use. If they were to be used for their intended purpose, someone would certainly have to wipe them down before they sat. A dozen green trash bags stuffed with who knows what were scattered around the floor of the porch.

I knocked on the door.

"Let me do the talking," I said, glancing at Shamrock standing beside me, still in his restaurant whites.

My friend looked grim, but he nodded rapidly. I knew he was pissed about what had happened to Dianne and he wasn't shy about punching someone in the nose if he felt they deserved it. But I didn't want to go that way. Violence would make the situation worse, and I hoped to avoid that by giving Sal a chance to return the goods, if he had them, or get them back if he didn't, in exchange for the police not being brought in. If Sal couldn't or wouldn't play ball, I wasn't going to threaten him. That might do nothing but involve Dianne, a prominent beach business owner, in an ugly incident. I couldn't have that. So the police would be our next step if it became necessary.

"Hey, there's someone inside," Shamrock said.

I turned, glanced at where he'd been looking. A shade was down and I couldn't see a thing.

Shamrock gently pushed me aside and rapped hard on the door with a big scarred fist. "I seen him, Danny. He peeked around the shade. Or someone did."

"Okay, okay," I said. "Take it easy."

Shamrock didn't take it easy. He banged again, harder this time. So hard I could see the wood door vibrate.

"I know you're in there, arsehole," Shamrock yelled. "I saw you at the window. Open the bloody door!"

He banged again. The door repeated its little dance.

I could hear someone shuffling about inside. Before Shamrock could continue beating the door, I threw an arm in front of him. "Hold it. Here they come."

A lock clicked, the knob turned, and the door opened a foot. A woman peeked out. She was young, maybe mid-twenties. It was hard to tell. She had some wear on her but she was still very pretty. Blue eyes and blonde, medium-length hair. She was the type you see often around the beach, especially in winter when the rents are cheap and you get a rougher crowd. That rougher crowd is usually tossed out by Memorial Day so the landlords can get the high summer rents, generally anywhere from $800 to $1,500 a week. The only exceptions were if the place was such a dump it would be impossible to rent to anybody except drunken underage kids. Some landlords didn't want to deal with that.

This had to be one of those situations. I couldn't think of any other reason a broke junkie house painter and his woman would be living on Hampton Beach during the expensive tourist season.

"What do you want?" she asked in a timid tone. I got the impression she had a general idea.

I cleared my throat. "We'd like to speak to Sal."

"He isn't here."

"Bullocks!" Shamrock said, shoving the door further open, the thin woman going along easily with it.

I reached to grab Shamrock's arm, but before I could get hold of him, he shouted, "There he is," and squeezed right through the door opening.

I went after him thinking of nothing except getting Shamrock out of the house. The last thing I wanted was a B & E rap.

The thin woman didn't try to stop me.

Standing off to one side was Sal Mariani. He was dressed in jeans and a ratty navy-blue Metallica long-sleeve T-shirt hanging loose at his waist. The room was what you'd expect—a mess.

"Oh, hi," he said, as he tried to cover the obvious fact that he'd been attempting to hide from us. "I told Tammy I didn't know who it was." Voice shaking, he added, "What's up?"

"What's up?" Shamrock bellowed. "Why you—"

I interrupted. "We want Dianne Dennison's jewelry back."

Sal was moving from foot to foot faster than a barefoot kid on hot asphalt in July. "Jewelry?" he said stupidly.

"You arse!" Shamrock shouted. He balled his fists and I could almost see the steam coming out of his red-tinged ears.

"Hold on," I said, giving Shamrock a look that I hoped told him I wouldn't be pleased if he kept up this tack.

The thin woman closed the door and stood with her arms squeezed across her chest, eyes turning nervously from Shamrock to her boyfriend and back again. She wore jeans low on her hips and a red long-sleeved top stretched tight over her breasts. Her face looked less worn when out of the harsh sunlight. She was even better looking than I'd first thought. I wondered for a moment what she saw in Sal Mariani. Then I realized. Drugs.

I looked at Sal. "Here's the story—"

"I didn't take no jewelry, Dan," he said, "I—"

I held up a hand. I didn't want to go down Shamrock's road. On the other hand, I wasn't going to play games with this loser either.

"Here's the bottom line," I began, "you've got twenty-four hours to get the jewelry back to her. Every piece of it."

"But I didn't take it." He lied about as good as a novice time-share salesman.

"I don't want to hear it," I said, waving my hand at the floor. "Twenty-four hours or we go to the cops."

"*Or* I'll beat your head in," Shamrock yelled. He shook his scarred fist again. His knuckles were bleach white.

I gave my friend a disapproving look. He stopped shaking his fist and came down off the balls of his feet.

Sal licked his lips, looked at his girlfriend. She looked disgusted. With him or with life in general, I couldn't be sure. Still, the look she gave her significant other told me this was probably her rented cottage, and she didn't want trouble here. It must have told him the same because he stopped protesting, looked embarrassed.

"He pawned them," the girlfriend—Tammy—said.

"I don't care what he did with them." Looking at Sal, I said, "You bring all of Dianne's property to the High Tide within twenty-four hours or I go to the Hampton cops and to my brother who's a detective on the state police."

I turned, pushing Shamrock in front of me, and headed toward the door. There wasn't a peep behind us.

Outside, we inched our way off the rickety porch and headed up the short street toward Ashworth Avenue.

"You think he'll come through, Danny?" Shamrock asked.

"If he can."

"You sound sure."

"Did you see the face on his girl?"

"Poor lassie tied up with him. She was pretty too."

"Whatever. I meant she gave him a look like she'll throw him out the door if he doesn't get the jewelry back."

"But he already hocked it."

"He can get it back. The pawnshops have to hold it for a while. And besides, he won't want any trouble with the cops. I'm sure they know all about him. This probably isn't a one-time thing by the looks of the whole scene. And remember what Eli said about him. The cops are certainly going to believe someone like Dianne over *him*, especially when Dianne tells them no one else has been in her place except Sal."

"How the hell did the dumb arse think he was going to get away with it?"

"Probably was desperate and hoped that Dianne wouldn't notice the jewelry missing for weeks if not longer. That way other people were sure to have been in her place, and he wouldn't be the only suspect. Luckily, Dianne opened her jewelry box sooner than he'd expected."

"What about you having a state cop brother?"

I shrugged. "Oh, I don't know. I just threw that in. In case Sal's not scared of the locals."

"I don't know if he's scared of them or not, but did you see how I put the fear of god into him, Danny?" Shamrock said, a big grin on his face. "That might light a fire under him too."

I shook my head, frowned. "You said you weren't going to do that, by the way."

"I know, I know," the Irishman said, suppressing his grin and letting a dark cloud form on his ruddy face. "But I just get so mad when I think of that freakin' junkie stealing from Dianne. We can't let him get away with it. That's all."

"He won't," I said.

We'd reached Ashworth Avenue. Before we turned and headed back toward Shamrock's cottage, he pointed up the street in the other direction. "Wally's?" he asked.

I thought a moment and then shrugged. Why not? I'd done all I could do concerning Dianne's stolen jewelry. For twenty-four hours anyway.

We started to walk in the direction of the popular biker bar.

"I need to call Dianne," I said. "Tell her we may have her stuff back soon."

It was almost evening and day-trippers were bumper-to-bumper trying to get to the bridge and off the beach. I didn't envy them.

Shamrock wiped the back of his hand across his fore-head. "I can taste that cold Heineken already, Danny."

"Just one though."

"Sure, okay. Just one."

Shamrock's little four-word statement was something I'd heard him or myself say many times before. And I knew it had about as much chance as coming true as the prediction from a beach fortune-teller. But I let it slide. That was part of the game we played.

Chapter 4

AND BOY, WHAT a drinking game it was. One I wished I hadn't played when the alarm clock went off the next morning at 9:00. I woke with a hangover that told me I'd be going through the motions today and that was about it. I had to work, so I struggled out of bed, afraid if I didn't, I'd drop off again.

I didn't look good in the bathroom mirror. My hair was spiked like a punk rocker's, and there were bags and dark circles under my eyes. I vaguely remembered that Shamrock and I had closed Wally's. That had to be about one a.m., their closing time. I assumed we'd walked home, even though I couldn't remember the walk. Nothing dark lingered in my mind to tell me anything unpleasant had occurred during the night. Nothing was out of order in the cottage, either.

At least that was something. Knowing the things that were possible, some of which had happened on my previous excursions with Shamrock, I considered myself lucky. So today I'd do what I had to do and start fresh tomorrow.

But right now I had to get ready for my day shift at the Tide. I did my bathroom chores, had a light breakfast of fruit and a bagel, and got dressed. I looked presentable enough for work—even though I felt the opposite.

Outside was hot and it was only mid-morning. The summer sun was bright, traffic was heavy already. I walked along in that nowhere state of mind that often accompanies a morning hangover. I hadn't been walking longer than five minutes and was just about to pop into Beverages Unlimited on the corner of M Street for a bottle of water when a Hampton police cruiser screeched to a stop at the curb beside me. Two cops were in it. I recognized both, though I didn't know their names.

The cop riding shotgun—the younger of the two—hopped out of the passenger seat, came around the cruiser toward me. He had no hat and wore dark shades. An elaborate tattoo peeked out from under his tight short-sleeve shirt.

"Dan Marlowe?" he asked. Before I could answer, he continued. "The lieutenant wants to talk to you."

I knew who *the lieutenant* was—Lieutenant Richard Gant of the Hampton Police. Right about now I felt like talking with Gant as much as I felt like having my teeth drilled. You see, Gant doesn't like me. Never has and never will. And that's downplaying it. The man has been convinced for years that I spent my leisure time thinking up crimes and scams to pull on Hampton Beach and the rest of the Seacoast and tries to prove his theory every chance he gets. I hoped this wasn't going to be one of those times.

I had no idea what Gant wanted, but I didn't hesitate to go for a ride. Hampton Beach was a small place, and I knew Gant could just walk up to the High Tide in an hour or so and harass me with whatever new crime conspiracy he'd dreamed up. And I also knew he wouldn't hesitate to bluster about my so-called crimes in front of my customers and co-workers. Better to go and see what the lieutenant with the tin foil hat wanted to accuse me of this time.

The tattooed cop opened the back door and I slid in. As I said, traffic was heavy, but it was moving. We were at the police station down back on Ashworth Avenue within minutes. The tattooed cop and I marched up the short set of stairs to the front door of the one-story cinderblock building and went inside. We walked down a corridor with bulletin boards plastered with local civic information lining each wall.

When we stopped in front of a door marked *Lieutenant Gant*, the tattooed cop gave it a rap. After a muffled voice answered, he opened the door a few inches.

"I got Marlowe, Lieutenant."

I was at an angle where I couldn't see inside but I heard Gant say, "Put him with the other one."

The tattooed cop led me farther down the corridor and stopped at a door marked *Interrogation*.

I was familiar with this room.

The cop opened the door for me, said, "Have a seat. He'll be right with you."

The first thing I saw when I walked into the room was the person I'd been with last night—Shamrock Kelly. He sat at a long metal conference table, dressed in his restaurant whites. He didn't look the worse for wear. I knew how much Heineken and Guinness he had consumed the night before and envied his tolerance.

"What the hell's going on?" I asked as I took a seat directly across from my friend.

Shamrock looked worried. "It's bad, Danny. Real bad."

"What happened?"

Shamrock's voice shook as he spoke. "They found Sal's body in the marsh at the end of my street this morning."

"What?" Now I was worried too. My hangover was on a back burner. Taking its place in my brain were visions of our visit to Sal's little hovel the previous day.

"They said his head was stoved in." Shamrock's rosy skin looked suddenly pale. "They picked me up at work and brought me here."

I was hoping that we'd been brought here because Shamrock's house was close to where the body had been found. I couldn't help but worry that it might have more to do with our visit to Sal's and things we'd said. Well, things Shamrock had said.

My blood pressure was up, and I felt the beginnings of an anxiety attack come on. I'd kept the attacks at bay for a long time, and they hadn't bothered me lately. I rarely took my medication anymore, but right now I wished the small prescription bottle was in my pocket instead of sitting in a drawer back at my cottage.

I tried to short-circuit the rising anxiety by surveying the room. I checked out the old black round clock on the wall, a few hanging framed pictures of local officials, and a map of the Town of Hampton on an opposite wall. I occupied myself for a short time studying the map. Much of another wall was taken up with a mirror. A mirror I assumed was one-way so suspects seated where we were could be watched anonymously. The only concession to the modern age in this interrogation room was a couple of cameras in corners near the ceiling. They were pointed at our table.

I was just debating whether the camera was on or if Gant was behind the one-way mirror studying us when the door opened.

Gant.

He had on a light blue short-sleeve shirt, red tie, and black pants. His iron-gray hair was combed straight back and he looked like he still worked out. He marched over to the table, sat at the head of it, and dropped a small stack of papers in front of him.

He folded his hands, elbows on the table, and looked first at me, then Shamrock, then back to me again. "You know why you're here."

It wasn't a question. Still, he seemed to be waiting for an answer.

When he was sure we weren't going to answer, Gant said, "What do you know about the body that was found in the marsh early this morning?"

"I don't know anything, Lieutenant," Shamrock said, fidgeting as he spoke.

Gant was silent for a short minute. His eyes narrowed as he looked at me. "Marlowe?"

I didn't like this but in a way I was glad for the conversation. It had taken my mind off my anxiety and derailed what might have been a doozy of a panic attack. "This is the first I've heard of it."

Gant banged the table so hard with his right fist that the papers in front of him fluttered. "Liars!" he yelled.

My heart jumped. This wasn't going to be any better than any of the other times I'd had run-ins with Gant. I could only hope it wouldn't be worse.

"Next you'll both be telling me you didn't know him." He fumbled around with the papers in front of him, yanked one to the top of the pile. "Salvatore Mariani's girlfriend says you were both at his home yesterday. *And* that you threatened him and tried to shake him down for money and jewelry."

"No, no way, Lieutenant," Shamrock said. He was leaning across the table toward Gant. My friend looked desperate,
something a fun-loving guy like Shamrock rarely was. "We
were just trying to get back Dianne's jewels. That scum . . .
ahh . . . that guy ripped 'em off."

"That's right," I said. I was surprised my voice sounded
firm. "He painted Dianne Dennison's condo and took some
of her jewelry along with his brushes and paint cans when he
left. We went down to get her stuff back."

Gant's lip curled. "And he wouldn't give it back, I'll bet.
So you . . ." He looked down at the paper in front of him.
"So you beat his head in as you threatened to do yesterday."

"We didn't . . ." I started, then changed my tack. "We
didn't mean it. We gave him twenty-four hours to return the
things he stole or we'd turn him into the police. Why would
we bother him before the time was up?"

Gant looked at me like I was a child rapist. "Because you
got tired of waiting or maybe it was just a line to get this Sal
Mariani to go out so you could grab him later."

His expression morphed into that of a man studying a
cunning animal. "Maybe Mariani was working for *you*. Or
maybe he fenced the stuff to *you*. This wasn't his first robbery.
But you'd know that. And maybe he got carried away and
couldn't resist keeping a few trinkets from your girlfriend's
place for himself. You wouldn't have liked that, would you,
Marlowe?" His eyes narrowed.

I wasn't going to just sit there and let this yahoo railroad
Shamrock and me into Concord State Prison. I had to speak
up and I did.

"And with hundreds of places on Hampton Beach we'd
take the body and put it at the end of Shamrock's street in
the marsh?"

Gant huffed. "Where were you last night?"

He was looking at me, so I answered. "I was at Wally's until closing."

"You?" he said, glancing at Shamrock.

He sighed. "I was with him."

Gant snickered, then said, "There's the answer. You both were cocked last night, got it into your heads you weren't going to wait twenty-four hours. You found Mariani on the beach somewhere, killed him, and because you were drunk, you stupidly dumped the body in your own backyard. Probably thought it would sink in the muck or maybe you were just too lazy to get rid of it somewhere else. And I bet you didn't bargain on an early riser notifying us about it at dawn either. Or that one of my men would recognize what was left of the face. And that we'd be interviewing his girl-friend while you were still sleeping off your hangover. Hah! You fucked up good this time, Marlowe."

Just then the door flew open.

"I heard that," the man standing in the doorway said. "Don't say another word."

"Connolly!" Gant said. "What the hell are you doing here?"

"The question isn't what am I doing here. What are you doing questioning my clients without their attorney present?"

Connolly's black hair curled in a wild Afro and he had on the usual rumpled suit I so often had seen him in. A battered brown attaché case hung from one hand. His eyes looked as wild as his hair.

I was sure that Dianne had called him. Whether she knew I was down here, or she thought only Shamrock was in the soup, I didn't know. Nor did I care.

"This is a murder investigation," Gant said.

"Are my clients under arrest?" Connolly asked.

Gant didn't respond.

James Connolly, attorney-at-law, scuffled around the table motioning with his briefcase for Shamrock and me to get up. As Gant didn't seem prepared to make any objections, we both rose. Using his briefcase, James herded us toward the door.

"If you want to talk to my clients again, Lieutenant, get in touch with me. I'll be glad to arrange it. In *my* presence."

I was a bit surprised that Gant didn't make a move to stop our exit, then remembered how he operated. He wasn't going to make a technical mistake in front of our lawyer, a mistake that could allow us to skate on this charge. That was how Gant thought. When it came to me, at least. He wanted me behind bars and had for a long time. And he'd messed up more than once where I was concerned. He'd make sure to cross his t's and dot his i's before he brought charges against us.

Outside in the broiling sun, Connolly was a ball of nerves. "Look, you two, I can't talk now. I'm going to be late for a case over in Hampton District Court. Gotta run. I'll talk to you later." He sniffled hard.

"Wait a second, James, what about . . . ?" I started but it was too late. Connolly was on the fly, heading for his old heap parked a short distance away. Over his shoulder he shouted, "And don't talk to Gant or any cops without me there. Ciao."

Shamrock and I just stood there.

"What now, Danny?" he asked.

"I don't know," I answered. And I wasn't lying.

Chapter 5

"WHY WOULD THEY dump the body at the end of Shamrock's street?" Dianne asked.

Dianne, Shamrock, and I were in her office in the back of the High Tide. Shamrock and I had just returned from our interrogation at the police station. Shamrock stood, leaning back against one wall. Dianne sat behind her desk. I sat in front of it.

"Coincidence," I offered. "Or *maybe* someone was trying to blame us?"

"I don't know, Danny. Why would anyone want to frame us for Sal's murder?" Shamrock asked.

I shook my head slowly. "I don't know. Maybe they somehow knew about our visit with Sal and they just took advantage of it."

"It's a pretty stupid thing to do," Dianne said. She was wearing a loose white restaurant shirt. She'd tied her black hair high in back, revealing a few strands of gray. "Who would believe you'd put a murdered body at the end of Shamrock's own street?"

"Gant," Shamrock and I said in unison.

"He'd believe anything about you—" Shamrock said, then quickly backtracked. "I mean us, Danny."

"Whatever," I said. I looked at Dianne. "I'm still going to get your jewelry back."

Dianne shook her head. A short black wave of hair came loose and fell across her forehead. "Dan, forget the jewelry. How can you even think of it at a time like this? You're a murder suspect." She raised her hand, pointed at me.

I reached over, took her hand, lowered it to the desk. "It'll be all right, honey."

Dianne looked at me like I was wearing a dunce cap. "All right? Didn't you hear what they did to Sal? To his head?"

She pulled her hand from mine and wrapped her arms around her chest, shivered. I saw her eyes water.

None of us spoke. What could we say to her? How do you soften the shock of someone you know being found with his head caved in and your boyfriend being accused of doing it? You couldn't. So we didn't try.

After a minute, Dianne made an attempt to bring herself out of her slump.

"It isn't good for business either, you two both working here." She attempted a not-very-successful laugh. Shamrock and I both forced a laugh, too. Our laughs weren't any more convincing than Dianne's.

Dianne looked at me, her eyes pleading. "Forget the jewelry, Dan. I'll get what I can through the insurance and call it a day. You can't be involved with any of this. Not with Gant after you."

"That's why I have to find your stuff," I shot back. "It's not so much the jewelry now. If I let Gant follow along on the trail he's headed on, he'll probably build some pie-in-the-sky case against me and Shamrock."

"You think he'd do that, Danny?" Shamrock looked about as uncomfortable as a Death Row inmate on the "Day."

I puffed out a little air. "You're kidding right?"

"Oh, Jaysus. He *would* railroad you . . . I mean, us, wouldn't he?" Shamrock's voice had risen an octave or two.

"He certainly would if we give him the chance. But we're not going to give him that chance."

Dianne leaned forward in her swivel chair, put her elbows on the desk and buried her face in her hands. "Here we go again."

She shook her head a few times, then held her hands out like she was begging. And maybe she was. "Can't you just let it go? Please."

I felt resigned to what I had to do and it showed in my voice. "We can't, Dianne. Gant's looking at me and Shamrock to hang this murder on. We're going to make sure he isn't able to do that. If we can."

"We?" Shamrock said.

"Yes, we," I answered, a little more loudly than I intended. I knew Shamrock wasn't trying to back out of the little adventure we were about to embark on. He'd follow me to the ends of the Earth if I needed his help, and he almost had many times in the past. He was just trying to steel himself for what might come. I knew that.

Shamrock pushed himself away from the wall, stood straight. "Of course I'll help you, Danny Boy. I'm involved too, after all."

"Yes, you are. It didn't help that you threatened Sal even after I told you not to."

"You threatened him?" Dianne said. Her face took on a whole new level of worry.

"No, no, no," Shamrock said. "I only said I'd sock him if he didn't get your goods back, Dianne."

"It was more like you said you were going to beat his head in," I offered. "Just like he ended up."

Shamrock shuffled from foot to foot. "I didn't mean it. Just trying to throw a scare into him."

"I know that," I said. "But Gant doesn't. What we have to do now is get our names cleared."

"How do you propose to do that?" Dianne asked. She was leaning back in her chair, staring at the ceiling, a look of resignation on her beautiful face.

"Sal's girlfriend."

Dianne stopped checking out the ceiling and eyed me like I'd lost more than a few points from my IQ. "You can't go near her. Gant would arrest you in two seconds."

"Maybe you're right. His girlfriend did say he pawned the stuff. Maybe that'd be a better place to start."

"What do we know about pawnshops, Danny? They're all over the place," Shamrock asked. "He coulda gone to Lowell or Lawrence. Or maybe even to Boston or Manchester. Where do we start?"

I shrugged. "I don't have any idea. But I know who might."

"Who?" Dianne asked as if dreading my response.

I was just about to answer when there was a tap on the door. It opened and Ruthie's face peered around the corner. "Dan, your favorite customers are here. And Eli's pissed already."

"All right. I'm coming," I said, getting up from my chair.

"I have to get some paperwork done, too," Dianne said. "If that's even possible under these circumstances."

"Talk to you later," I said before leaving.

"Bye, Dianne," Shamrock said. "I'm going home for a bit of sleep."

"Please, take care of yourselves. Both of you," Dianne said. Then in a quick afterthought she added, "and don't pursue this because of my jewelry. It's not that important. Believe me."

"We're involved now, Dianne," I offered. "We'd have to follow it through no matter whose stuff it was."

Outside in the short corridor leading through the kitchen and beyond, Shamrock asked who I had in mind to ask about the pawnshops. The kitchen was busy with Guillermo, the head chef; a new kid doing prep work on the speed table; and a couple of waitresses heading to and from the dining room, so I said, "I'll have to tell you later."

When I finally told Shamrock who we were going to see he wasn't happy about it.

Not happy at all.

Chapter 6

"DANNY, WHY THESE two arseholes again?" Shamrock asked. "Isn't there anybody else we can go to?"

It was the following day. We were in my green Chevette and had just driven over the Hampton Bridge on our way to see the two "arseholes" in question. "These are the only people I know who'd be familiar with which pawnshops local junkies sell their stuff to."

I glanced at Shamrock sitting beside me in the car. He looked as dejected as he sounded. "I guess you're right. It's just that every time we get involved with them . . . I don't know . . . something bad happens."

Trying to cheer up my friend, I said, "We don't have to worry about that this time. Something bad has already happened. What else could go wrong?"

Shamrock quickly made the sign of the cross. "Ahh, please don't jinx us, Danny. I'm worried enough as it is."

"Nothing to worry about, Shamrock." Of course, I was lying. There was plenty to worry about. A bludgeoned body, for one. And someone trying to pin the murder on me and Shamrock. We both had to keep our cool in trying to unravel this mystery without making matters worse than they already were. If that was even possible.

We were both silent the rest of the short drive, and it wasn't long before we turned into a mobile home park in Seabrook and followed the winding road to the end. I pulled up to a well-maintained trailer home at the end of a tiny cul-de-sac and beeped the horn. Shamrock sulked beside me.

"We're taking them with us?" he asked.

"I told them I would. They haven't got a car and this is the only way they'd agree to help us."

We sat and sat. Shamrock reached over and laid on the horn. I had to finally remove his hand.

"The damn eejits," he said.

Just then two men popped out of the front door, jogged down the steps, and opened the car's back doors.

I turned to look at them. "Hi, Eddie. Derwood."

"Dan, my man. It's good to see you," Eddie Hoar said as he climbed in behind Shamrock.

"Hey, Dan, long time no see," Derwood Doller said. The car rocked as the big man settled into the seat directly behind me. "Hey, Shamrock."

Shamrock grunted.

Eddie was still Eddie—cheap gold neck chain and disco clothes that went out of style back in the late 1970s. His unnaturally dark, black hair was slicked back on his head. Anybody could see that he either used a lot of cheap gel or he rarely washed his hair. Whatever, I was getting a whiff of a familiar odor I didn't like. His incessant snapping of chewing gum only added to my uneasiness.

Derwood hadn't changed much either, if at all. Still a big lummox, who favored jeans and old T-shirts. I guess you could describe him as sloppy casual. His hair looked as if his barber had used a bowl to shape it.

"Where are we going, Eddie?" I asked.

"Where are we going? We're going to a pawnshop that everybody on the Seacoast uses. That's what you wanted to know, isn't it?" Eddie was fidgeting around like he had a flaming hemorrhoid.

"They handle hot stuff?" I asked.

Eddie's pockmarked face looked a lot like a weasel's would if one wore clothes. "Of course they do. With the right people. That's why you need me." He thumbed his scrawny chest. "They know and trust me."

If they handled hot goods, I had no doubt they knew Eddie. I did doubt the part about trusting him though. People on the Seacoast who trusted Eddie were few and far between. Eddie and Derwood were small-time beach con men and petty thieves. Always had been. Everyone knew to check their medicine cabinets after these two used their john.

Shamrock and I had found ourselves mixed up with the pair during various beach shenanigans a couple of times in the past. They wouldn't harm a fly, but they weren't harmless, either. Their scams and schemes seemed to bring trouble to whomever was around them at the time. At least that's what Shamrock and I had found out. We tried to stay away from associating with them as often as possible.

But this time I had no choice. I had to find out quickly where Sal had pawned Dianne's jewelry. It wasn't only about the stolen goods, though. I also had to find out what happened to Sal—at least enough to clear Shamrock and myself. And who better to ask than Eddie Hoar?

When you're looking for a bottom-feeder, you have to use a bottom-feeder. Right?

"Where to, Eddie?" I asked.

"It's an easy one, my man. Right over on Route One. Salisbury."

Shamrock harrumphed. "I thought we were going down to Lawrence or something. Salisbury? We coulda found that ourselves, Danny. We don't need these two."

Eddie leaned forward, putting his head between the two of us.

"Hold on just one minute. The owner won't trust you. You look like a cop," Eddie said to me. Then perusing Shamrock's white uniform, he added, "And you look like an ice cream man."

"Shut your mouth, arsehole," Shamrock said, face reddening.

Eddie sat quickly back. "You'll need me if you think she's gonna tell you about hot stones."

"He's probably right," I said to Shamrock, who seemed to be debating whether to go over the seat and have at Eddie. My words seemed to put the brakes on him a bit. Before I turned back to the wheel, I pointed at a large brown bag on the seat beside Eddie, a bag he'd brought from the trailer.

"What's that?" I asked.

"A VCR," Eddie answered. "A nice one too. Figured I'd do a little business while we're there. You know, kill two birds with one rock."

"It's stone, moron," Shamrock said.

"That better not be hot, Eddie," I fired off. "We don't want to get in any trouble. We've already got enough."

"It ain't hot," Eddie said indignantly. "It's my aunt's."

"She knows you're going to pawn it?"

"No, but we do it all the time. Don't we, Derwood?"

"Yeah all the time . . . at least until we can't get it out of hock and she finds out, like the time we took her antique love seat and—"

Eddie interrupted. "Shut up, Dumwood."

"Don't call me that, Eddie. You know I don't like it." Derwood reached across and grabbed Eddie's pencil-thin neck with his hand. He must have squeezed because Eddie's small dark eyes bulged and he gurgled.

I leaned back over the seat and grabbed the big man's arm, trying to break his grip on Eddie's throat. I couldn't, but Derwood let go anyway. Eddie rubbed his neck and manipulated it from side to side.

"Can't you take a joke, for Chrissake?" Eddie said, his voice a bit hoarse.

"I don't like you to call me that, Eddie. I told you a million times."

"Forget it," I said, disgusted. I turned back to the wheel, started the car. "Route One. Right?"

"That's what I said, Jack." Eddie answered.

Shamrock gave Eddie a threatening glance. "Don't get smart, arsehole. You respect my best friend. His name ain't Jack."

Shamrock turned forward, watched me maneuver the car down the winding road leading out of the mobile home park. "It oughta be Mr. Marlowe to the likes a you."

The ride was uneventful accept for Eddie cajoling the story of Sal Mariani's death out of me, as we drove from Seabrook to Salisbury.

When we reached our destination, Shamrock said, "How come all the places like this pawnshop, dirty book stores, strip

Chapter 7

THE STRIP MALL Eddie had directed us to was on Route One in Salisbury. It looked like dozens of other strip malls that dotted the congested road all the way from Salisbury, Massachusetts, through New Hampshire and beyond that into Maine.

I pulled in and parked at the far corner of the mall in front of a laundromat. The pawnshop was at the other end of the long building and I wasn't sure I wanted anyone to get my plate number.

In addition to its name, *Seacoast Hawk Shop*, painted on the facade, the shop also had an electrified sign hanging in the front window flashing the words *Cash—Gold—Pawn* on and off rapidly. The rest of the mall housed a video rental store, an electronics store that oddly advertised "Dart Supplies," and a convenience store.

"All right," I said reluctantly. "Let's go."

I was uneasy about going into any business establishment with Eddie. But my desire to clear our names trumped my doubts. "And, Eddie, let me do the talking."

clubs, and fireworks stores all seem to be either in Seabrook or Salisbury? We're always ending up in one or the other."

"Something in the water?" I offered.

But I didn't believe it for a minute. There was more to it than that.

A lot more.

"I'll have to do some groundwork for ya, Dan," Eddie responded as we all scrambled from the car. "This dame will clam up, if I don't."

I grunted. Unfortunately, Eddie was probably right. I looked uneasily at the bag in Eddie's hand as the four of us trooped over to the pawnshop door. For some reason, I wasn't surprised when opening the door triggered a few verses from the song, "Money," by Pink Floyd.

Inside, the shop seemed to peddle everything but the kitchen sink. I assumed I'd probably see that, too, before long. Hanging on the wall was a large moose head with a dangling price tag on it. On either side of the moose were two extension lamps with their glare directed onto the dead animal. The lamps also had price tags as did almost everything I could see. I'm not going to tell you what else was hanging on the walls. There was so much junk there, I'd never get this story told if I tried to describe it in detail. Enough to say a lot of it *was* junk and more than a lot of it looked ridiculous.

Glass display cases were crammed everywhere in the small shop. In fact, there were so many and placed so close together, you had to turn sideways to get around them. Their contents were more interesting than the wall displays though. Each case seemed to hold one type of item: coins, watches, small collectibles, and a few that held jewelry. I didn't get much of a chance to check out the jewelry cases as I would have liked to. Eddie maneuvered around the display cases like he'd done it many times before and headed for the rear of the store where a woman stood behind a counter. I knew I had to be there when he spoke to her.

I chased Eddie, catching up to him just as he reached the woman. I was afraid to let him alone with her for even a minute. Never knew what he might say without Shamrock or me looking over his shoulder.

Shamrock and Derwood had been distracted by the display case that was holding the coins.

"Hey, Selma," Eddie said. "How's my favorite lady today?"

I pegged Selma at about forty or fifty years old, and she looked like she'd lived every minute of it. Her hair was dyed jet black and she wore bright red lipstick along with dark red splotches of rouge on both cheeks. Her silk-like blouse was so large it could have passed for a car coat the way it draped on her heavy body. She wore more jewelry than a maharaja— large turquoise rings, necklaces of gold and silver. So many bracelets hung from both wrists I was surprised she could lift her arms. A pair of glasses hung from a thin chain around her neck. Another neck chain supported a jeweler's loupe.

"Whaddaya got, Eddie?" Selma responded, and by the not-too-friendly tone of her voice I could tell Eddie was anything but her favorite guy. "I haven't got all fuckin' day."

"Yeah, yeah, sure, Selma." Eddie pulled a VCR from the bag, placed it on the counter.

"That again?" Selma rolled her eyes. "Pawn as usual?"

Eddie nodded rapidly.

"Forty bucks as usual." Selma said. Her ringed hands grabbed the counter as she looked intently at Eddie.

"Sure, sure, Selma. That's fine."

Selma picked up the VCR and walked to the end of the counter where she scribbled on some forms.

While she was occupied, I whispered to Eddie, "Let me do the talking. You just tell her I'm okay if she asks." After seeing Selma's reaction to Eddie, I wasn't sure that would do me much good, but it was all I had.

"Don't worry, Dan," Eddie said, throwing his shoulders back and smiling like a crocodile. "You're with Eddie Hoar here. You saw how she loves me."

"Yeah, I did. That's why I hope I don't get tossed out on my ear."

Eddie chuckled like I'd been joking.

Selma finished her writing and returned to us. She handed Eddie forty bucks, a receipt for the VCR, and a form for him to sign. When that was all done, Selma said, "Anything else?"

"My business associate here—" Eddie began before I interrupted him. Any hint that I worked with the likes of Eddie Hoar could be the kiss of death as far as getting information from Selma.

"I talk for myself, Eddie," I said as I elbowed him aside and stood directly across the counter from Selma. Her perfume was overpowering but not as offensive as her breath. Blessedly, she pulled back a bit.

I decided to play it semi-straight with Selma, instead of using Eddie for a reference. "We're not business associates . . . we were both just coming this way."

Selma eyed me suspiciously. "So whaddaya want?"

I cleared my throat. "I was wondering if you had a fellow named Sal Mariani in here recently?"

Selma's eyes narrowed. "I don't talk about my customers," she said. Then added quickly, "Not that he ever was."

"And he won't be now either," Eddie spit out. "They found him offed over in Hampton."

I glared at Eddie, wanting nothing more than to throw him through the front door. Not that I didn't think Selma already knew about Sal's untimely death. I was sure she did;

it had been publicized after all. I just didn't want it brought up that way, didn't want to spook her.

Eddie must have picked up on my anger because he looked embarrassed and quickly scurried back to the display cases where Shamrock and Derwood were still oohing and aahing over the coins.

I turned back to Selma. "Look, Selma. This Sal character stole some of my friend's jewelry. I just want it back. I won't cause any trouble. We might even come to some agreement on me buying it back."

Her tone became syrupy. It sounded strange coming from someone who looked as hard as she did. "I don't have your friend's jewelry, sir. We don't *ever* handle stolen merchandise or do business with known thieves."

How she could lie like that was beyond me. But I had to play the game if I hoped to get anywhere. Which meant I had to slow down. At least for now.

"Red there works over the High Tide in Hampton, don't he?" Selma said before I could reply. She was looking over my shoulder at Shamrock and Derwood who stood near a display of VCR tapes and small electronic equipment.

"Yes. How'd you know?" Then caught myself. "Oh, his work clothes," I added, referring to the restaurant whites Shamrock always seemed to be wearing.

Selma gave me a smile as phony as a hundred-dollar Picasso. "I've seen him there before. Goin' from the kitchen to the men's room."

I couldn't remember ever seeing Selma at the Tide, but then again, there were probably lots of occasional customers I never saw. Especially at night. And Selma didn't look like the type that got out much.

"Ahh, yeah," I said, "but if you think of anything that might help me, could you give me a call?"

"Of course, I'd be happy to, sir," she said as if she were a teller in a bank cashing an important customer's check. It was damn unnerving.

I snatched a business card from a little plastic holder on the counter. "Do you have a pen?"

Selma retrieved a pen from under the counter. I wrote the High Tide's phone number on the back of the card. I thought it best to keep my own number—and the address connected to that number—out of Selma's hands. Since she knew where Shamrock worked, it wouldn't be hard to connect me to the Tide. So that number was compromised all ready.

Selma accepted the card without looking at it and made it disappear down below where the pen had materialized from.

"Thanks for your help." I nodded, gave her a half-wave, and turned to leave. As I passed Derwood and Shamrock, I muttered, "Come on, let's go."

They followed me through the maze of display cases and out into the sun.

"Where's Eddie?" I asked.

"There's the fool," Shamrock said, pointing to my car. Eddie's flat head was visible in the back seat.

The three of us trooped to the car and took up our previous positions.

"Why'd you leave, Eddie?" I said, looking at him in the rearview.

Before Eddie could answer, Derwood said, "He wanted to get out of there before Selma saw what he swiped. Right, Eddie?"

"Shut up, Dumwood."

"I told you I don't like that name, Eddie."

Before Dum . . . err . . . Derwood could follow through on what looked like it was going to be a head slap, I turned. "Knock it off, you two. I'm not putting up with this shit. Not at a time like this."

Derwood, who'd raised both his body and his hand, relaxed back into the seat. Eddie looked everywhere but at me.

"What did you take, Eddie?" I asked.

"I didn't take anything, Dan. Honest."

"Honest? That's a joke coming from you. Show me or I'll let your friend have his way."

"He won't have to," Shamrock said. "I'll be happy to do it." Before I could react, Shamrock was half over the seat, his beat-up knuckles bouncing off Eddie's skull.

Eddie threw up his hands, trying to protect himself. "Okay, Okay, I'll tell ya," he squealed.

I grabbed Shamrock's arm and pulled him away from Eddie. Eddie rubbed his head. I was sure he'd have a few lumps tomorrow.

"Geez, I was only kidding. I was going to show you guys when we got out of here."

"Sure you were, Eddie. What'd you take?"

He lifted his skinny ass off the seat and rummaged around in his back pocket. When his hand came out, there was a small ring sitting in his palm. I reached for it. Eddie pulled his hand back.

"Gimme that, Eddie, or I'll let Shamrock and Derwood both take a poke at ya."

"That'd be a pleasure," Shamrock said. Derwood grunted.

Eddie reluctantly handed over the ring. I studied it. Maybe a small diamond wedding ring.

"How'd you get this?" Everything I'd seen had been locked in display cases—except for the larger items hanging on the walls.

Before Eddie could answer, Derwood piped up. "He swiped it right out of the case. Didn't ya, Eddie?"

Eddie scowled.

"Weren't the cases locked?" I asked, looking at Eddie in the back seat then at the ring in my palm and back again.

"Eddie can open them with a paperclip," Derwood said.

"A paperclip?" I said.

Derwood nodded. "Eddie can open 'em fast too. Fifteen seconds is his record, huh, Eddie? Did you make a new record this time?"

"Why don't you tell everyone my skills, Dum . . . err . . . Derwood? Once everyone knows, they aren't good anymore."

"I saw a camera in there, nimrod," Shamrock said. "She's probably got you on tape."

"No, Eddie's too smart for that," Derwood said. "He knows where the cameras are pointed."

Eddie seemed to like the compliments. He smiled. "There's only two, and they don't move none. One's pointed at the register and the other at the front door."

"I oughta give you two black eyes," I said. "Now take this ring back and return it one way or the other. Put it back in the case if you have to."

Eddie got jittery, waved his hands in front of him. "I can't do that, Dan. She'll watch me the minute I come back in. She'll know I been up to something."

"Give it back to her then."

Eddie shook his head in short little bursts. "She'll call the cops, Dan. We'll all get in trouble. And she'll never have nothin' to do with you again either. You won't find out anything about your chick's jewelry."

"Great!" I said. "I should slap you silly."

Instead I started the car and headed away from the Seacoast Hawk Shop. I had a feeling I'd see Selma and her business again. If luck was on my side, it wouldn't be because of Eddie's thievery. It would be something a little more beneficial to my investigation.

Chapter 8

AFTER GETTING RID of Eddie and Derwood, I dropped Shamrock off at his place. I didn't have to work, so I retreated to my cottage and made an early night of it. An early night for me at least. Had a few beers, of course, but that was it.

The phone rang just after midnight. I stumbled out of bed in the dark. Disoriented, I walked face-first into the wall adjacent to my bed, hitting the wall hard. I'd never done that before. I grabbed my face, feeling blood trickling between my fingers. Stunned, I fumbled for the light switch, then grabbed a towel hanging on a hook on the back of the door and put it to my face. The phone was still ringing.

I cursed and went to answer it.

"Hello," I said, none too friendly.

"Danny, my house is on fire!" Shamrock yelled. I could hear sirens over the phone.

"What?" I said.

"My, my house, Danny. It's on fire."

My heart started slugging against my chest. "Are you all right?"

"I'm all right . . . but my—"

"Where are you, Shamrock?"

"I'm at my neighbors, but I'm going back now."

"I'll be right there."

I hung up, dashed for the bathroom. The towel I held to my face was splotched with blood. In the mirror I could see the blood pumping from a nasty gash near the bridge of my nose. My forehead and nose looked a bit swollen but were secondary worries now. I had to stop the blood flow.

The first Band-aids I used were as effective as trying to stop a dike leak with a toothpick. Looked like I might need a stitch or two to close the wound, but I didn't have time for that luxury now.

I put the towel back to my face, went to the bedroom, and managed to get dressed. I wouldn't be able to park anywhere near Shamrock's right now. Not only was it summertime, which meant parking wasn't easy, but the street would be blocked off by cops and fire apparatus by now.

I headed down my dark street on foot, holding the blood-soaked hand towel to my nose. Surprisingly, it didn't hurt.

There were enough sirens you'd think the Casino building was on fire. Then again, any house or business fire on the beach brought a heavy firefighting response with fire equipment coming in from surrounding towns. A lot of the beach—cottages, motels, and other businesses—had been constructed at the turn of the century and were made out of wood. And because Hampton Beach was just a little strip of land between the Atlantic Ocean and a salt marsh to the west, buildings were built very close to one another to get the most use out of the land, there being few, if any, zoning laws in the early years.

That's why no one fooled around when there was a fire on Hampton Beach. If the wind caught the flames in a

certain way, you could lose the whole damn beach. There had been major fires in the past that wiped out many homes and businesses alike.

I crossed Ocean Boulevard and headed down a side street leading to Ashworth Avenue and Shamrock's street. I reached Ashworth, my suspicions confirmed by the sight of a fire truck and two cops blocking Shamrock's street. The cops were directing traffic. There was some smoke in the sky over Shamrock's house. I zigzagged around the cars that were moving at a snail's pace.

I reached the corner of Shamrock's street and my heart skipped. The walls of Shamrock's cottage were standing and the roof looked okay, but firemen were pouring water from their hoses through what had once been windows. There were no flames, but lots of smoke. A crowd had gathered around, watching the firemen do their thing.

I looked around for Shamrock but didn't see him anywhere. A few people stared at me and I suddenly remembered I had a bloody towel to my face.

"Danny, Danny." My Irish friend bounded off the porch of the house next to his. He pushed his way through the throng of people and came up to me. His face was redder than usual. If I hadn't known better, I'd have thought he was out of breath. He had on a white T-shirt, baggy brown shorts, and dirty sneakers. His hair was sticking out in all directions.

"Jaysus, Danny, my house. Look—" He stopped and studied me, eyebrows furrowed. "Are you all right, Danny?"

I nodded.

He didn't ask me what happened, just said, "Are you sure?"

"I'm okay, Shamrock. Just banged my nose."

He must have accepted that explanation because he turned toward his cottage. "Sweet Mother of Mary. My fucking house."

It was my turn to ask, "Are you all right?"

"Aye, I'm fine, but just barely." He looked back at me, his eyes glistening. "They burned my house, Danny. They burned my goddamn house."

I gave my friend a hug. We didn't do that often, and I felt him tense a bit. I pulled away. "What do you mean *they* burned your house?"

He looked troubled, almost frightened. "I was asleep, Danny. I heard an explosion in my living room. I jumped out of bed, looked in. Fire was going right up the walls. I couldn't do a damn thing. I barely got out the door."

He'd been talking in an excited rush and stumbling over his words, so I could imagine how close it had been. Shamrock never had any problems talking.

I was just going to ask him again about the *they* he'd mentioned when Lieutenant Gant bulled his way through the crowd and marched right up to us. He was wearing a black leather car coat and had a younger detective in tow.

"Kelly, I want to talk to you." He said it in a tone a cop generally reserved for a criminal suspect.

Then, as if he just realized I was there, he turned to me. "Of course *you're* here, Marlowe." He nodded at Shamrock. "You this guy's landlord? This an insurance scam?"

I was stunned. Gant thought I was capable of a lot, but to torch a house with my friend in it? "Are you crazy? Shamrock was in there when the fire started."

"That's what you say," Gant said, a snide little look on his face. I wanted to rip that face off his skull. "Or maybe you

two were just trying to cover up evidence, maybe something concerning Mariani's murder?"

"We didn't have anything to do with his murder," I said.

Gant furrowed his brows and pointed at the towel I was using to dab blood from my nose. "What's that? You cut yourself somehow torching the place?"

"You *are* crazy," I said softly.

Gant either didn't hear me or chose to ignore the comment.

"What do you say?" Gant turned his hard gaze back to Shamrock.

"What . . . wha . . ." Shamrock stuttered.

A uniformed cop strode up. "Guy was drinking on the porch across the street, Lieutenant. Saw someone come up from between the burnt cottage and that one." He pointed toward the cottage where Shamrock had waited for me. "Whoever it was lit a Molotov cocktail and heaved it through the front window, then beat feet back behind the cottage. Probably ran over to the next street."

"He give you a description?"

"Young guy, he thought. Jeans, T-shirt. That's all he could tell."

"Anything else?" Gant asked sourly.

The uniform shook his head. "He ran inside to call the fire boys. When he came out, he saw this man running out the front door." He pointed at Shamrock.

"All right," Gant said. He didn't sound happy. "Question all the neighbors, see if anyone else saw something."

Shamrock and I didn't speak, just turned back toward his cottage. Except for some dark gray smoke kicked up by the water still being laid down, it looked like it was just about over. Firemen entered through the front door.

"What *did* happen to you, Marlowe?" Gant asked suspiciously.

"I got in a fight with an orangutan," I said without looking at him.

"Don't get smart with me."

"I wouldn't think of it."

Gant finally wandered away. Shamrock and I stood there for a while.

What the hell was going on?

First, a painter murdered and dumped at the end of Shamrock's street. Now, my buddy's home had been firebombed.

Coincidence?

Or something else?

Chapter 9

THE FIRE HADN'T done as much damage as we'd feared, probably because the firehouse was located only about one hundred yards from Shamrock's home. The living room walls had been scorched and some furniture destroyed. Shamrock had already spoken to his landlord. Repairs were to start right away and might be completed within a short time.

That meant I had a houseguest.

"I tell you, Danny, you had a premonition. You sensed I was in danger, even though you were asleep, and that's why you banged your nose."

I was sitting in my favorite chair. Shamrock was on the sofa. A large bandage decorated the bridge of my nose—a gift from Exeter Hospital where we'd stopped after leaving the fire scene. No stitches but some kind of glue crap they used to close the wound.

"I don't think so," I said. "I think I just got up beer-dazed and confused by the phone and walked into the wall."

Shamrock had been excused from work for the day, and I still had time before I left for my late morning shift. We were attempting to process what had happened.

Shamrock smiled and shook his head very slowly. "Danny, Danny. Your people have been here a couple of generations so you don't remember, but back in the 'Ole Sod' they say people can sense when family or close friends are in danger. And we *are* close friends, Danny."

My turn to smile. "We are that but . . ."

"Ahh, Danny. How many times have you gotten out of bed and almost busted your beak?"

He had me there. Besides, if my best friend thought our friendship was so strong that we knew when the other one was in danger, why would I ever want to diminish such a noble notion? There were stranger things in life, many of them not so nice. So I changed the subject.

"We have to get to the bottom of this, Shamrock."

Shamrock wrung his hands. "Who in the name of all that's holy would burn me out of house and home? Who would do such a thing?"

I didn't answer.

"Any ideas at all, Danny?"

I thought of Selma and how she'd recognized Shamrock from the High Tide. Would she go that far—firebomb a home with someone asleep in it? And if she had—why? Certainly not over a little jewelry. If it had been Selma, or someone she'd sent, there had to be something a lot more sinister going on.

"Possibly Selma over at the pawnshop," I said.

"Aye, I was thinking that too." Shamrock furrowed his red brows. "But why would she do that, Danny? She could have . . ." His shoulders went up a bit, and he shuddered.

"Looks like we stumbled onto something a lot bigger than Sal selling her a couple of rings."

"There's got to be more than we know about," Shamrock agreed. "Otherwise, only a nut would do something like that."

The sounds of footsteps thumping up my porch steps caused us both to turn toward the front door. Seconds later, someone knocked. I rose, went to the door, and unlocked it. Locking my door was a habit I'd gotten into years ago when break-ins had become much more prevalent on the beach. My home had even been entered once while I slept in the bedroom. They'd rifled the pockets of the pants I'd left strewn across the living room sofa. They'd gotten no more than a few bucks. That was the end of unlocked doors at night.

I swung the wooden door open. In front of me, on the other side of the screen door, stood a stranger. He wore the thickest glasses I'd ever seen. Otherwise, he was ordinary in features, size, and clothes.

"Can I help you?" I asked.

"Are you Dan Marlowe?" His voice was as ordinary as the rest of him.

"Yes," was all I said.

"Can I talk to you for a minute?"

"About what?"

"Something for your benefit, I assure you."

The man looked as threatening as Mr. Rogers, so I opened the screen door and motioned for him to come in. He did, tripping over the lip of the floor as he entered. I caught his arm. It was thin.

I pointed to the chair in the corner, the one beside my easy chair.

"Something to drink?" I asked. "Water, tonic, beer?"

He shook his head as he took his seat.

I thought it best not to introduce Shamrock until I knew why the man was here. I sat and waited for him to speak. Shamrock looked apprehensive.

The man cleared his throat. "I've come here for a friend, Mr. Marlowe."

"Dan's fine," I said. "And who are you?"

The man nodded. "That's not important. Yesterday you visited my friend's business. You upset his wife."

I noticed that not only were his glasses as thick as the often-mentioned Coke bottles, but the center of each lens had a funnel that appeared to be some type of magnification gizmo.

"The pawnshop?" I asked.

"Yes, Seacoast Hawk Shop." The man took a handkerchief from his back pocket, mopped his brow. It *was* getting hot in here. Summer, after all, and the early morning coolness was already burning off. "Well, the thing of it is . . . you made my friend uncomfortable."

I fought the urge to jump in. It would be better if I played it cagey and let this character tell his entire story.

When I didn't speak, Mr. Glasses continued. "You were bothering my friend's wife. Asking questions. Disturbing her."

I had to respond to this. "We weren't disturbing her. My girlfriend had some jewelry stolen, and I think it was pawned there. Selma didn't seem too bothered to me."

Mr. Glasses wiggled his hand in the air. "Whatever, Mister . . . ahh, Dan. You made her very uncomfortable. My friend would like to it to stop." He hesitated, added, "Or there may be unpleasant consequences."

Shamrock, who'd been silent up until now, finally spoke up. "You come here and threaten us, you arsehole? After what you did? I'll . . . I'll . . ."

He leaped out of his seat, headed for our visitor. I jumped up and held Shamrock's arm just as he was about to grab the man's shirt. The man reared back, his eyes huge behind the odd spectacles.

"Jesus, Shamrock. That won't do any good. And we don't know for sure." I held his arm until I felt his muscles loosen. I eased Shamrock back toward the sofa and he retook his seat.

I sat down again. "You'll have to excuse my friend. There was a fire at his house last night. An *intentional* fire." I scowled at the man as I spoke. Whether he could see me clearly or not, I didn't know.

The man seemed to relax a bit. "I don't know anything about any fire," he said.

"Like hell you don't," Shamrock said. He started to get up again. I motioned him down. He sat back sullenly.

I tried to keep my voice calm. "What is it you want?"

The man didn't seem quite so confident now. He kept glancing at Shamrock as he spoke to me. "My friend would like you to stay away from his business and stop bothering his wife. That's all."

I was a bit bothered myself but tried not to show it. "We weren't bothering his wife. I told you, I was just trying to get my girl's stolen jewelry back."

The man studied me for a short minute. At least I think he was studying me. I had no idea how clearly, if at all, he could see my features. Finally, he reached into the right front pocket of his pants and removed a black velvety pouch. He held the pouch up. The words *Seacoast Hawk Shop* were stenciled on the pouch.

"This is what you were looking for, I think," the man said.

I reached for the pouch. He pulled his hand away.

"I'd prefer to dump the contents out and take the bag with me, if you don't mind."

I didn't mind. I grabbed the large ottoman sitting on the floor between me and Shamrock and slid it closer to our guest. He promptly dumped the pouch's contents on the flat surface.

I recognized the earrings I'd given to Dianne. The rest— rings, bracelets, and necklaces—I had no idea if they were hers but assumed as much.

As Shamrock and I looked at the jewelry, the man said, "There, that ought to make you happy."

"Is this everything that was stolen?" I asked.

"As far as I know," he answered. He hesitated as he continued, "So . . . that will be the end of you bothering my friend's wife and disrupting his business?"

I scooped up the jewelry and placed it on an end table beside me. "I can't promise that."

"Why?" he said, voice rising. "You've got your friend's jewelry back. What more do you want?"

There was still the murder of Sal the Crapper left unsolved.

But I thought it unwise to let this man know that. I had no idea if this little theft was all that he, Selma, and her husband were hiding. "I'm just not promising anything."

"And we're gonna find out who burned my house and almost killed me. You can be sure of that," Shamrock said, his tone menacing.

The man sounded nervous now. "I don't know what you're talking about. I don't know anything about any fire." He took out his handkerchief again. This time, he removed his glasses and used the cloth to rub sweat from his eyes. His eyes had the strange, tired look peculiar to long-time eyeglass wearers when they remove their specs. Only his eyes looked ten time worse.

"Did you want anything else, Mr . . . ?" I said.

"No, nothing," he said, shaking his head rapidly. "You've got the jewelry back. My friend went to a lot of trouble to get that stuff for you, and you should appreciate it. There's no need to go back and disturb them. They are very busy people."

On the outside chance that the pawnshop owner either hadn't, or at least hadn't knowingly, acted as fence for Dianne's jewels, I grudgingly said, "Thanks."

The man got up from his seat, returned the pouch to his pocket and headed for door. "Good day."

After he clomped down the porch stairs and the last sound disappeared, Shamrock said. "I hate to admit it, Danny, but Eddie was right. They bought Dianne's jewelry from Sal."

"Apparently. Anyway, we got it back." I glanced at the loot on the end table. "I hope it's all hers, and it's all here."

Shamrock leaned forward, his forearms on his knees. "They musta burned my house trying to scare us off."

I wasn't sure. "I don't know, Shamrock. Why would they try something as serious as arson and risk mur—"

I stopped cold for a moment then resumed. "Then try something easy and relatively risk free like returning Dianne's jewelry just to get us to stop nosing around? Wouldn't it be the other way around?"

Shamrock slumped back on the sofa. "Aye, Danny, it would seem that would be the way to go about it. But if they didn't spark my place, who did?"

I didn't know. All I knew was that this visit from the man with the strange glasses wouldn't have any effect on Gant's suspicion that Shamrock and I were involved in Sal's murder. Completing our own investigation to clear our involvement in that murder trumped everything else in importance.

That's why I couldn't let this go. Didn't matter that Dianne's jewelry had been returned. If we didn't find Sal's killer, I might be spending the rest of my life sharing a cell in the state prison with Shamrock. And even though I liked him a lot, I'd pass on that.

Chapter 10

LATER THAT AFTERNOON, I stood in front of Dianne's desk in her office at the High Tide, looking at her seated behind it. She had on a white work shirt. Even though it was loose, her breasts still pushed against the fabric.

I opened the clear ziplock bag I'd brought with me and carefully let the jewelry trickle out onto the desk. Rings, bracelets, necklaces, all of it. The jewelry looked impressive even though I knew Dianne had said the entire boodle was only worth a couple of thousand dollars.

"Is everything there?" I asked.

She used a forefinger to poke around the jewelry. "I think so. I can't be sure, though. Some of my stuff I haven't worn in years." She was silent for a bit, then added, "I guess it's all here. At least everything I care about."

"You're sure?"

She shrugged. "As sure as I can be. How'd you get it back?"

"The pawnshop owner where Sal sold it brought it back to us."

"He just gave it to you?"

"Well, yeah. He sent someone with it. He didn't want trouble over a few rings and things."

Dianne looked at me sternly. "You didn't go over there and threaten him, did you, Dan?"

I acted shocked. "Me? Threaten someone? No."

She pursed her lips. "I hope not. Some of the people that run those places look kind of rough."

"I guess."

"So everything's okay now. Right?" She arched her thin brow.

There was no air conditioning in Dianne's small office, and I was hot. I could feel little rivulets of sweat running down my back. Not just from the heat. I was nervous too. Dianne could read me like a book. I wasn't sure I could fool her.

"Dan? What's the matter?"

"Nothing, honey."

She folded her arms and sat back in her swivel chair. Her breasts jutted out further, and the chair squeaked.

"I'll *honey* you," she said. "Now what's the matter?" She held up her hand like a cop stopping traffic. "No, don't tell me. You're still going to try to find out who killed Sal. Aren't you?"

I shifted from foot to foot. I couldn't lie to Dianne. She knew me too well. Knew *almost* everything about me. She was my girl and I wanted to do my best to keep it that way.

"Gant's still trying to hang the murder on me and Shamrock."

Dianne leaned forward, elbows on the table, and stared at me hard. "So? You two didn't do anything. It's not like he hasn't tried to get you in trouble before. He just likes to scare you, Dan."

"Dianne. This is *murder*."

"Like I said, so what? You and Shamrock didn't have anything to do with that little thief's death. And everybody knows it. Stay out of it!"

I tried a soothing tone. "If I don't do anything, Gant will hang it on us."

"Bullshit!"

"Dianne, come on. Even if he can't prove anything, Gant will be all over the beach asking questions, all with my name attached to them." I got desperate, played a trump card. "I've gotten my good name back . . . *mostly* . . . in the past few years. I can't risk losing it again."

Dianne leaned forward, steepled her fingers under her chin, and looked at me. She was a bit calmer when she spoke. "You poking around will lead to trouble, Dan. It always does."

"Not this time. I promise." I couldn't tell her about the veiled threat Mr. Glasses had made at my cottage. She'd hit the roof.

"How can you promise something like that? You can't." She gave me a funny look. "What is it, Dan? Tell me."

Boy, could she read me.

"Nothing, nothing," I said, shaking my head rapidly. Then tried to change the subject. "What about Shamrock's house? Someone tried to burn it down. And they almost killed him! I have to help him find out who did that. I owe him a lot, Dianne. You know that."

She did. Shamrock had saved my life more than once during various incidents we'd been involved in over the years in Hampton Beach. To my advantage, Dianne was very fond of Shamrock. Not only because of the good friend he'd been to me, but also to her. Not to mention that she'd known Shamrock since he first came to the beach from Ireland many years ago as part of a wave of temporary beach workers that had come for the summer. Unlike the rest of the summer help that year, Shamrock had never left. Like Dianne and I, he'd fallen in love with Hampton Beach.

"I hope that doesn't have anything to do with Sal's death." She seemed resigned now to meeting me in the middle.

"I'm sure it doesn't," I half lied.

"Why don't you let your lawyer handle this problem with Gant?"

"Connolly? I don't know if that's wise." I was thinking about how Connolly had sniffled the last time I'd seen him. Even something as innocuous as that sniffling had triggered my bowls to growl and unpleasant memories to return, memories of my own cocaine abuse.

Dianne, of course, knew about my past history. "Oh, come on. That was a long time ago."

A nice attempt but, I could detect a little nervousness hidden between the words. I didn't want her to lose her confidence in me, so I said, "All right. I'll see if I can get him to get Gant off our backs."

"Good." She smiled. She had beautiful teeth and a great smile. The camera loved her, as they say. And so did I.

She reached down, picked up one of the earrings I'd bought for her. With her other hand she very slowly pushed her hair out of the way and attached the earring to her small lobe.

"You're going to put those on now?" I asked, clearing my throat.

"Just for a little while, Dan." Her green eyes suddenly seemed greener and the office grew even hotter.

She took the other earring from the desk and repeated the process on her other ear. Her neck was taut and turned toward me. When she faced me again, her lips were moist.

I came around the desk, reached for her hands, and pulled her to her feet. I gazed into those green eyes for a long moment before I drew her to me. Her breasts gave a little against my chest. I kissed her full lips, and our mouths opened. Our tongues danced. There was the taste of mint in her mouth. The anxiety of what had been going on the last couple of days and how I felt about Dianne made certain I didn't need much foreplay. She knew it; she could feel it. After a minute, she pushed me away.

She was flushed and when she spoke her voice was husky. "For god's sake, Dan, let me lock the door."

I released her. She went, threw the small bolt lock on the door, came back, and this time she tore right into me. We kissed deeply, almost angrily, exploring each other's bodies with our hands. That didn't last more than a couple of wonderful minutes before we were in a frantic race to get the other's clothes off first.

There was a small couch in Dianne's office. It was the best option; we'd used it before. And we used it again.

Chapter 11

IT HAD BEEN good, as it always was with Dianne. We had only a minute to catch our breaths before someone tried to open the office door.

"Dan, they want you at bar," Guillermo said in accented English.

"Okay, I'll be right there," I said, my voice cracking.

Dianne and I clumsily got to our feet and quickly put our clothes back on.

"Great," Dianne whispered as she hooked her bra and then struggled back into her white work blouse.

"It's only Guillermo," I said, almost losing my balance putting my shorts on.

"Shh, shh," Dianne put a finger to her lips.

When we were both back to normal and Dianne was behind her desk pretending to peruse her papers, I muttered, "See you later."

"We're not going to do that here again," Dianne said softly.

"I know. We won't." I threw the little bolt and stepped from the office.

As I closed the door behind me, Dianne said, "You always say that."

And you do, too.

I stormed through the kitchen, ignoring Guillermo, and the others. I pushed through the swinging doors, hurried through the dining room, and rounded the partition that separated the room from the bar area. The first people I saw were my two regulars. Paulie sat in his usual place, near the front window at the end of the L-shaped bar. Eli also sat on his customary stool, near the middle of the bar directly in front of the beer spigots.

I went around to the business side of the bar. Eli was puffing furiously on a Camel cigarette. Of course, he was the first to speak. "Chrissake, you're late again! We thought they still had you in the hoosegow."

Paulie piped right up. "*You* said that. I didn't say a thing."

So they had heard that I'd been down at the police station. That wasn't surprising; neither of them missed much about Hampton Beach goings-on. Paulie usually kept his mouth shut when it came to information that might be uncomfortable to someone, like me for instance. Eli—far from it. He thrived on gossip.

I glanced at the Budweiser Clydesdales clock over the back bar. It was 11:05. I was five minutes late. To Eli, that was as bad as an hour. He was on the most regimented beer schedule I'd ever known. Paulie was a close second. I got a draft Bud for Eli; Miller Lite, no glass, for Paulie. Then I ran around trying to get caught up on my bar prep chores. It was helpful to keep moving. If I stopped, Eli would have something to say about the scuttlebutt he'd obviously heard.

By the time they were halfway through their second beers, I'd run out of work to do. I'd barely leaned my butt against the backbar to take a breather when Eli spoke up.

"So the cops think you and the Irishman had something to do with Sal the Crapper's death?"

He didn't beat around the bush, did he?

"No," I lied. I was desperate to short-circuit his interrogation. If Eli got going, he might still be talking about it when the bar was full, which would be soon. This was the last subject I wanted to get into with customers.

My lie didn't do any good. It had been a long shot anyway.

"No? The whole beach knows they had you two down there and they was asking you questions. Did they use a rubber hose on ya? Ha, ha, ha."

Paulie hadn't said anything yet. He'd let Eli lay the whole ugly thing out so he wouldn't be blamed for any unpleasant fallout. Paulie bided his time, blowing perfect smoke rings that rose and broke one after the other on the ceiling.

It was useless to hope Eli would drop the subject. He never had before.

I sighed. "They just wanted to ask us if we knew anything about what happened to Sal."

Eli leaned toward me, almost sticking his head between two of the beer spigots. "What did ya tell 'em?"

"We didn't tell them anything. We don't know anything."

Eli shot back on his stool, straightened his scrawny body. "Whaddaya mean you didn't tell them anything? Didn't you tell 'em that little bum stole your girl's jewels?"

I sighed again. "Of course I told them that. But he probably stole from half the people on the beach."

Eli's eyes narrowed. "Yeah, but you and the Irishman were plenty pissed-off."

I didn't say anything.

Eli must have picked up on what I was thinking. "Course I'd never tell the cops any of that. My lips are sealed." He made a motion with his finger across his mouth.

Paulie guffawed. He knew as well as I did that to seal Eli's lips someone would need super glue.

I folded my arms across my chest. "Look, they're questioning a lot of people on the beach."

I didn't really know if they were questioning anyone else. If they were, they were probably asking questions about me. Still, my main interest right now was to get Eli off the subject. "A lot of people probably had it in for the guy. You said yourself he was a thief and junkie."

Eli threw his shoulders back indignantly. "Yeah, but I didn't threaten him."

I got a little hot and showed it in my tone. "And I didn't either."

Eli lowered his voice a bit. "Well, that there's in the ear of who's listening. The bum never stole nothin' from my girl."

Paulie couldn't resist. "That's 'cause you never had one."

Eli looked at him. "I had plenty of women in my day. You'd be surprised. And I don't see you with any playmate on yer arm."

Paulie flicked an ash off his butt into the tray. "I had one. That was enough."

I knew that was an uncomfortable subject for Paulie, so I was surprised he'd gone there. His girlfriend had died unpleasantly years ago. No one ever wanted to talk about it. And no one did.

Silence filled the bar. I dreaded hearing Eli pick up the Sal subject again but was saved from his questioning when a group of town workers jostled their way through the front door and headed for the bar. They spread out on stools between Eli and Paulie.

Eli wouldn't try to talk to me while I was moving, doing business. The busier I looked, the less likely he'd be to talk to me. So I kept myself very busy with the town employees.

As I did, I realized that I had been right in deciding to get to the bottom of who killed Sal Mariani. If Eli and Paulie knew, then it wouldn't be long before the rest of the beach would be aware that Dan Marlowe, former owner of the High Tide Restaurant and Saloon and recovered cocaine addict, may have slipped back into his old ways and gotten himself in deep trouble. If that happened, my ex-wife would find out and there would go my visitation rights with my two kids. I couldn't let that happen.

Chapter 12

I COULDN'T WASTE any time in my search. I had the next day off from my bartending duties. I waited until Shamrock had returned after his early morning shift. He usually went to the Tide before dawn where he did a cleanup, general maintenance, and the everyday chores that were needed to get a popular resort bar and restaurant ready for another busy day. Often he stayed late to run the dishwasher during the lunch rush. On this particular morning, a summer worker took over the dishwasher job. Shamrock was back at the cottage by ten a.m.

I'd gone easy on beer the night before and had gotten in my morning run on the beach. I was seated in a porch rocking chair when Shamrock turned down the walk and headed for my cottage.

"Hey, Danny, nice day, don't you think?"

"Yeah, Shamrock, you ready to go?"

"You got your panties in a twist, eh? I got time to drain my vein?"

Minutes later, the two of us were on the Hampton Bridge, whizzing along in my little green Chevette.

Shamrock sat in the passenger seat puffing on a butt. I rolled down my window and glanced at him. The cigarette had a wet lip on it, as usual. Shamrock was very hard on his smokes.

"Where are we headed, Danny?"

"Back to Seacoast Hawk Shop."

"We've already been there. It'd be dangerous and a waste of time going back. You ain't got no new ideas?"

I slowed as I passed the Round Rock Restaurant and O'Keefe's General Store and took a right onto Route 286. Already the traffic heading in the opposite direction, toward the beach, was backing up at the lights. It would get a lot worse. It was going to be a nice beach day.

"No, I don't. And we're just going to observe this time. No one will know we're there. Besides, it's the only shady connection we've got with the painter."

"Yeah, but there's probably many others, Danny."

"You've been asking around, right?" He'd told me earlier he was going to.

"Yes, I have. You know I would have told you if I heard anything. The gobshite was a junkie and sneak thief, just like we thought. I didn't hear anything about anybody wantin' to smash his head in, though. But he could have stolen from the wrong person or ripped-off a dealer or something, I guess."

Sure, he could've, I told myself. But Shamrock was like the Mayor of Hampton Beach. If anyone forgot to brush their teeth in the morning, he'd know it. My friend would've picked up on animosity bad enough to result in Sal's murder. Yet, Sal was dead.

"Maybe, but until we hear something like that, we're going back to stake out our only lead," I said.

Shamrock brightened.

"Stakeout?" he said. "I like the sound of that. Like two private eyes, Danny. You can be Jim Rockford and I'll be Colombo. I like that little guy, he's slyer than a leprechaun."

"But he's not a P. I., he's a cop."

Shamrock frowned. "Oh."

He thought for a moment, then snapped his fingers. "I know, I'll be that Magnum guy. The ladies like him, and he lives in Hawaii, and he's always driving that fancy sport car. What kinda car *was* that, Danny?"

"I don't know," I said, shaking my head. "It wasn't his, anyway. His boss's or somebody's." I shot a quick look at Shamrock, "But you do look like him. Except for maybe your red hair. But if you dyed that?"

"Ahh, Danny, you're pullin' my joint again." A second later, "You are, aren't ya?"

"Me?" I said, shrugging my shoulders. "Course not. There's a strong resemblance. Maybe he's Irish, too."

"You ain't kidding?" Shamrock leaned forward and turned the rearview mirror so he could study his face. I glanced at him a few times. When he was done, he swung the mirror back into position and relaxed.

"Maybe there is a little resemblance," he said.

I reached up and adjusted the rearview into its correct position, just as I made the turn into the parking lot of a car wash adjacent to the strip mall where the pawnshop was located. I pulled over to the far right. The pawnshop was on the other side of some bushes that ran almost the length of the property line between the two businesses. Our car was partially concealed by the bushes, and we'd have a good view of the front door of the pawnshop.

I'd used this car wash many times through the years. It wasn't one of those automatic ones where your car was pulled through on tracks and washed. It was the type with various bays that you drove your car into, tossed some coins in a slot, grabbed a wand and did the wash yourself, which meant they often had no attendant.

Today there was one lone car being washed by its owner. I'd been right about the attendant. None in sight.

I reached behind me and retrieved a pair of binoculars. I generally used them to study the Isle of Shoals, boats, and other things off the coast and remembered to throw them in the car before Shamrock had showed up at the cottage. I leaned a bit forward to see around Shamrock, put the binoculars to my eyes, zeroed in on the shop's front door, and adjusted the lenses. A couple of guys were walking in, both carrying bags.

Over the next couple of hours, there was a steady stream of customers, and it didn't take long to realize that more merchandise seemed to be going into the store than coming out. For every three people that entered carrying a box or bag, only one—at most—came out the same way. Obviously, this enterprise was buying a lot more than it was selling.

Shamrock and I traded the binoculars back and forth between us. By the third hour, Shamrock had grown tired of playing private detective.

"Let's get out of here, Danny," he said, sounding weary. "We get the idea. They're pawning a lot of hot stuff. We already knew that. This is gettin' us nowhere."

"Hold this," I said, taking the binoculars from my eyes and shoving them in Shamrock's hands. A car had pulled into the lot and was cruising slowly by the pawnshop. It went the length of the building, disappearing around a corner toward the rear of the structure.

I opened my door, jumped out.

"Hey, where you going?" Shamrock shouted.

"I'll be right back," I answered. I jogged along the bushes marking the property line toward the back of the buildings. When I was opposite the rear of the strip mall, I crouched and duck-walked until I could see the car I'd just spotted driving through the lot out front.

The driver's door opened and out stepped a big man wearing a sport coat and sunglasses. He held onto the door and looked all around him. I couldn't see him too well, but I had the feeling I had seen him before. I'd made a mistake not bringing the binocs.

When he was apparently satisfied the coast was clear, he closed the car door gently and entered what I was sure was the back door of the pawnshop. My first thought was to get Shamrock down here with the binoculars. Considering Shamrock's extensive familiarity with seacoast residents, he might be able to peg who this visitor was.

I was on my way back to the car when I heard the squeal of tires. A car came to a fast stop behind my Chevette. I hurried back to the car, reaching it as two men got out of the car stopped behind mine. I jumped in the driver's seat, hit the door lock, and quickly rolled up the window, relieved there was nothing in front to block me in.

Shamrock had already done the same.

One man came to Shamrock's side, the other to mine.

"Roll down your fuckin' window," the man on my side said.

I couldn't get a look at the man on Shamrock's side—his head was above the car window—but the face of the guy on my side told me he'd be right at home in a cell block at the state prison. On his large head was a blue Union Army cap.

"What do you want?" I asked.

He made a rolling motion with his hand. "I just want to talk to ya a second."

Sure he did. And I just wanted to get my car washed. Still, maybe I could bluff my way out of here. I rolled my window down, stopping about halfway.

"All the way, asshole," he shouted. A tattoo, along with lots of black hair, peeked out from the neckline of his black T-shirt.

"No. What do you want?" I asked again.

"What are ya doing spying on the businesses here?" He nodded toward the strip mall.

I was just about to lie, when Shamrock shouted, "Tire iron!"

I glanced in Shamrock's direction in time to see a hand—holding a tire iron—on the other side of his window. I grabbed for the ignition key, but the ape beside me had reached in and was trying to get to get to the key, too.

Glass exploded on my right and Shamrock screamed. I went for the window handle with my free hand and cranked the window closed as rapidly as I could. When I had the Ape's arm trapped, I used both hands to crank the window even tighter.

"You motherfucker," the Ape screamed, continuing to bat at me with his trapped hand.

I protected my face with one arm and glanced at Shamrock. The passenger window had been completely shattered. Shamrock had both arms over his head and was cowering sideways toward me. The punk who'd shattered the window had an arm inside, trying to get the door open.

I turned back. The Ape had his fire-engine red face almost pressed against the glass. He was shouting obscenities at me.

I started the car, rolled down my window and thrust the palm of my hand in the Ape's face. He staggered backward, grabbing his injured arm.

I dropped the car into drive and floored it. We peeled out. The punk on Shamrock's side was holding the inside door handle. We dragged him with us. I swerved around the back of the car wash and floored the car again. It was a fairly wide lot, and I got going pretty fast. The punk was afraid to let go and was screaming his stupid head off like a little child. I smiled as I stomped on the brakes. He went cartwheeling across the asphalt, bouncing nicely. I came around the front of the building and didn't even stop when I pulled out onto Route One. There were a couple of angry horns, but we got onto the road without a collision, headed in the direction of the beach.

After a couple of minutes, I slowed to a normal speed. Shamrock and I had both gotten our emotions somewhat under control.

"For the love a Mary," Shamrock said. "That was close."

"Not only don't they want us visiting the place," I said, "it looks like they don't want us watching the comings and goings at Seacoast Hawk Shop either."

Shamrock picked at the front of his clothes, removing shards of glass.

"You didn't get cut, did you?"

"Nah. I was lucky. Coulda lost a peeper." Shamrock gave the front of his white restaurant shirt a final brush with his hand. "By the way, what did you see out back? Anything?"

I'd almost forgotten about the man behind the store. "Someone went in the back door of the pawnshop. Checked out the whole area before he did."

"He see you?"

"No." I thought a moment. "But he did look familiar. I was coming to ask you to take a look at him when he came back out, but those two gorillas put the squash on that."

"Too bad, Danny," Shamrock said. "If he hung his knickers anywhere around here, I surely would have known him."

I smiled. "That's what I figured, Shamrock."

"Hey, wait a minute. I just thought of something. You don't think those goons followed us to the shop, do you, Danny?"

I hadn't thought of that. It was possible. But it was just as possible they had been guarding the hock shop and spotted us.

"Maybe. Or maybe they picked up on us here."

"What now, my man?"

I honestly had no idea, and that's what I told my friend.

"Well, Danny, don't worry. You always have a knack of coming up with something."

I wasn't sure about having a knack, but I knew I had to come up with something. And fast.

Chapter 13

I DIDN'T WASTE much time thinking about our next move in solving this riddle of robbery, arson and murder. I didn't have to. The next step presented itself to me. Or more correctly—to Shamrock and me.

It was around 9:30 that night. We were in my cottage—Shamrock on the sofa, me in my easy chair, as usual. Both drinking Heineken beer. The windows and doors were open, letting in the warm breeze. I hadn't heard any noises outside except the usual cacophony of summer beach sounds.

The first hint that something was out of the ordinary was the sound of multiple people storming up the steps to my front porch. If I hadn't been pretty clean for a while, I would have assumed it was a drug raid.

When the screen door yanked open and two men burst in, I almost wished it had been a drug raid. The first man through the door had a gun in his hand, and it was pointed at me. I recognized the second man right away. It was the Ape whose arm I'd closed in my window. The man—he really did remind me of an ape—didn't appear to have a weapon, but his arm was heavily bandaged, and he didn't look too happy about it.

I glanced toward the bedroom where my shotgun hid under the bed. There wasn't a chance I could make it.

"Don't move a fuckin' muscle, either of ya." the first man said. He didn't need to say it. It all had happened so fast that Shamrock and I hadn't had time to do anything but turn toward the door. Now we sat like two stone statues.

"Close the door," he said to the Ape.

When the first man came through the door, I hadn't noticed anything about him except the automatic he held in his fist. Now I took stock of the guy. He was a big man, like his gun. Over six feet tall. A little overweight, but you could see that there was a lot of muscle underneath. I pegged him at 250. You definitely wouldn't want him on top of you if you happened to find yourself in a fight at the local dive bar.

His ugly face was plastered on a head the shape of a cinderblock. It looked like it had taken quite a few whacks through the years. His hair was either dirty blonde or just plain dirty gray. I couldn't be sure. A toothpick jutted from between his lips, bobbing up and down as he spoke. I figured him for about forty, give or take five years. He wore a ratty gray sweatshirt with the arms cut off at the biceps, cheap jeans with the legs whacked off at the knees, and sneakers that many years ago had probably been white.

The two of them stood there for a short minute. By now I figured Toothpick was the man who had smashed the passenger window earlier. The road rash on his legs and arms confirmed it. He glared at me. "What the fuck you doing, Marlowe, nosing around the pawnshop?"

How could I answer that one? I couldn't deny it. Yet I was hesitant to say we were hoping to find whoever was responsible for a murder. I had visions of me and Shamrock being zipped up in body bags.

My anxiety was on overdrive but I had to keep it at bay. "We were looking for a couple of rings that were stolen from my girlfriend."

"Bullshit!" Toothpick snapped. "You got all that stuff back."

"There were a couple missing," I said, my voice cracking.

"Like hell there were." Toothpick's voice was still raised, but not as much, and I detected a tiny bit of doubt in his tone. He turned and looked at the Ape.

I did too. In addition to the blue Union Army cap and the abundance of black body hair I'd noticed earlier, the Ape's arms hung very low at his sides. The guy even moved like a gorilla. If you ever doubted the theory of evolution, the Ape was sure to burst your bubble.

"He's lying," the Ape said. "He got it all back. The little man handled all that."

He hesitated a moment, then asked, "Think he'd take a coupla pieces for himself?"

Toothpick exploded in laughter, almost losing his toothpick in the process. After he resituated the toothpick between his teeth, he said, "You're shittin' me. That little weasel is scared to death of me."

The Ape guffawed. "Your wife, too."

Toothpick half-turned the gun on his partner. "Shuddup, Georgie."

Georgie the Ape glanced at the gun, then back at his companion. "Sorry, boss. I forgot."

"Don't forget again." Toothpick turned the gun and his eyes back to me but only for a second before he switched his attention to Shamrock. "You gonna tell me why youse was sneaking around the pawnshop and eyeballing it, mick?"

Shamrock cleared his throat. "Like he said, we were look-ing for a couple of rings that his girl didn't get back from that little weas . . . ahh, I mean that little guy."

"They're lying," Georgie said softly.

"Maybe," Toothpick answered.

"They know something, I tell ya."

"Maybe."

"They ain't gonna stop nosing around."

"Maybe."

"Let's do 'em."

"Maybe."

That was it. "Now wait a minute. You guys are blowing this all out of proportion. We were only looking for the two missing rings, but if it upsets you so much, we'll forget about them and you'll never see us again. Right?"

I looked at Shamrock. His complexion was greenish-white. He just nodded. I assumed he was too scared to speak.

"I don't believe youse," Toothpick growled. He pointed his gun at the windows that faced the street and the dunes beyond. "Them dunes would probably be a nice place to bury a body or two. Don't ya think?"

I could swear I heard Shamrock gulp. I suddenly won-dered if I could bribe Toothpick into letting me retrieve a Xanax or two from the sock drawer in my bedroom. And maybe I could reach my shotgun at the same time.

"It's summer," Georgie said. "Lotta people around."

"Sure, but not at three in the morning. We could put 'em down a couple a feet real fast. Take no time at all. Or . . ." An ugly smirk came across Toothpick's face. "Or we could just do 'em here and leave 'em for his girlfriend to find."

Toothpick snickered. "You know, two in the old melon."

Georgie guffawed again.

I had no idea if they were bluffing or not, but it didn't much matter. If we told them we were surveilling the pawn-shop to find out who murdered Sal the Crapper, we might very well be signing our death warrants.

I had two choices—either stay with the story I had told them. Or tell them the truth. It was a flip of the coin as to which explanation held the better odds for our survival.

"Give. Now!" Toothpick said in a guttural voice, shaking the gun at me.

I was just opening my mouth to speak, when the porch steps thundered again. For the second time that night there was a knock at my door.

The others turned, stared at the door. I looked at Toothpick. He stepped over to me, leaned down.

"Get rid of whoever it is." He jiggled the gun in my face as he talked, then straightened up and motioned for Georgie to follow him into my bedroom. They had a view of us from where they stood.

I got up, went to the door, and opened it. Standing there was someone I was rarely thrilled to see. This time, I wouldn't have been happier if it was the Reader's Digest man with the giant check.

Chapter 14

EDDIE HOAR STOOD on the other side of the screen door. Behind him, shifting from foot to foot, was the big lummox, Derwood Doller. I was surprised to see them. I couldn't remember either of them being at my house before. And I say *remember* because there was always a possibility they had been here before. Many pieces of my past from back in the day were missing from my memory bank.

I was glad to see them, to say the least. Maybe Toothpick wouldn't be so fast to shoot Shamrock and me with two other people in the cottage. Then I realized that Toothpick might think nothing of killing four people as easily as he did two. I couldn't risk that. Not even with Eddie and Derwood. I had to get them out of here.

"Hey, Dan, how ya doing?" Eddie said. "We was in the area and thought we'd drop by for a visit."

I didn't believe that for a second. Yet I didn't have time to wonder what foolishness had really brought these two clowns to my door. "Look, Eddie, I'm busy now. I'll talk to you later."

"Gotta girl in there, huh?" Eddie said, a dirty little grin on his face. "No problem, we just gotta talk to you for a minute. Then you can go back to your . . . ahh . . . activities."

"Yeah, sure, that's it . . . a girl," I said. "I'll talk to you later."

As I started to close the door, Eddie craned his neck, peering around me into the living room. "Hey, there's Shamrock. Come on, Derwood."

Eddie reached for the screen door handle. I made a grab to lock it, but Eddie was too fast. He yanked the screen door open and shoved past me. Derwood followed reluctantly behind him.

Once inside, Eddie bobbed his head up and down, looked at Shamrock and said, "Hey, man, how ya doing?"

Shamrock mumbled something. He didn't look good.

"What's the matter?" Eddie said, suddenly looking apprehensive. Apparently, he'd picked up on a bad vibe. The man was street smart. But he was too late.

"I'm what's the matter, pea-brain," Toothpick said from the open doorway of my bedroom.

Eddie spun around. He lost at least two shades of color and his beady eyes suddenly became big. "Ponzie!" he said, his voice sounding as if he'd just bumped into the father of a young girl he'd raped.

Ponzie stalked into the room, the Ape right behind him.

Eddie gulped. "And . . . hi, Georgie." Eddie sounded even more frightened.

"I ain't surprised a punk like you'd show up here, Hoar," Ponzie said. "But you picked a real bad time."

Eddie stared at the big gun in Ponzie's hand. "Yeah, yeah, sorry about that, Ponz. Me and Derwood'll just come back some other time." Eddie took a step backward.

"Shuddup and sit down," Ponzie growled. Eddie looked around, probably seeking an escape route. Not finding one, he nodded at Derwood. They both took seats beside Shamrock on the couch.

"Close and lock the door, Marlowe."

I did.

Eddie leaned over to Shamrock and whispered, "What's goin' on?"

Shamrock leaned away. "Don't even talk to me, you arse."

"I told you not to come in, Eddie." I said. "You screwed up this time."

"He always screws up," Shamrock said in a tone that told me my friend was resigning himself to his fate.

I still wasn't convinced that this Toothpick guy—this Ponzie—was actually going to kill us all. He was most likely bluffing, at least he had been before Eddie and Derwood had shown up. If it had been anyone other than these two beach hustlers, I would've figured it even less likely we'd be killed.

But Eddie and Derwood didn't lower our chances of being killed, not one bit. Eddie had a rather-large stable of sea-coast people who would like to see him dead. The fact that he knew Ponzie wasn't going to do us any good. In fact, with Eddie's rep for ripping people off, our odds of not living long had just increased.

"Get back in the chair." Ponzie nodded at me and I re-took my seat.

Georgie stood just behind Ponzie. Eddie gulped but said nothing. I wondered if the fireworks were about to start or if Ponzie was going to resume his questioning. Fortunately, it was the later.

It was unfortunate, though, who he picked as his target. He walked over to Eddie, leaned down so he was in his face.

"Whaddaya know about these two casing my business?"

Eddie seemed to shrivel. "Me, Ponz? Nothin'. Nothin.'"

Ponzie furrowed his brows. "What the hell's this?"

He grabbed a thick, gold-colored chain with an emerald marijuana leaf that hung from Eddie's neck. He peered at it, then looked at Eddie with eyes that were mere slits. "Why, you fuckin' asshole!"

He ripped the chain from Eddie's neck as Eddie yelped.

"You ripped that off from my store," Ponzie growled.

Eddie held up his trembling hands, palms out. "No, I didn't, Ponzie. I didn't. I bought it on the cheap from—"

Ponzie cut him off before Eddie could throw someone, deservedly or undeservedly, under the bus. "Bullshit, worm! Now I got a good reason to give to you what I was about to give to your friends."

"No, Ponzie, please—"

"Shuddup! You tell me what they was doin' eyeballin' my shop." Ponzie stood straight, put the end of the gun barrel against Eddie's forehead.

Of course, Eddie started blabbing his fool head off. Anyone might, I guess, but Eddie would have done it even if a gun hadn't been involved, so it didn't count for much in his case. "They wanted to get Dan's girlfriend's jewels back. Sal Mariani ripped 'em off. They thought he sold them to you."

"I wonder how they got that idea." Ponzie gave the gun a nudge and Eddie's head rocked back.

Eddie stuttered, "Not . . . not . . . me, Ponzie, honest. Not . . . not . . . me."

"They got the swag back. So why would they be checking the shop out? Talk. Fast!"

Eddie looked desperate. I hoped he wouldn't say anything too damaging, but that was wishful thinking. "They probably wanted to know who whacked Sal. Yeah, that's probably it, Ponz. They did say something about that."

"You little rat," Shamrock said, raising his fist.

"Knock it off, mick." Ponzie took the gun from Eddie's forehead. It left a deep red indentation. Shamrock lowered his fist, glowered at Eddie.

"Why would they think I had anything to do with that?" Ponzie continued, keeping his eyes on Eddie.

"I don't know, Ponz," Eddie said. "Crazy, I guess."

Ponzie chuckled, looked toward the Ape. "Whaddaya think?"

"Let's do 'em all," he said. Whether this was a bluff or not, I still didn't know, but I was a lot less sure than a while ago.

"Now wait a minute, you guys," Derwood said as he started to rise from his chair.

Ponzie pointed the gun toward him. "Sit down, big boy, unless you wanna be first."

Derwood plopped back down.

"Last chance," Ponzie said, looking around at the four of us. His eyes stopped on Eddie. He must have known if we were hiding anything, Eddie would be the weakest link.

He was right. Eddie spoke rapidly. "It's in his bedroom somewhere."

"What's in his bedroom?" Ponzie said warily.

"Evidence. Yeah, that's it. Some kinda evidence he said he had. Ain't that so, Derwood?"

Eddie elbowed Derwood and he stuttered, "Err . . . yeah . . . yeah . . . sure, Eddie. That's what he said."

I knew there was no evidence in my bedroom. Eddie was stalling.

Ponzie muttered to the Ape. "Give the room a good toss."

The Ape—aka Georgie—went into my bedroom and began rifling through my drawers.

Just before all hell broke loose.

Chapter 15

EDDIE HOAR WAS closest to the door and farthest from the window. Ponzie swung his gun on me and a split second later, Eddie made his play. If I hadn't seen it with my own eyes, I wouldn't have believed it.

Eddie leaped off the sofa like he'd been catapulted. He took two giant steps toward the window and dove. The dive was so perfect, I could've been watching an Olympic diver going through my open window, pushing the screen in front of him as he went. Ponzie swung his gun toward the window, but it was too late. A thud sounded below on the sand along with a scream. Then the sound of feet running down my walkway.

Would Ponzie have fired if he had a shot?

I'll never know. Neither will I ever know if he really meant to kill us or if the threats had been a bluff all along. If he had intended to kill us, Eddie doing a swan dive and escaping had short-circuited that outcome.

Georgie came in from the bedroom. He appeared puzzled as he stared at the screenless window. "What the fuck happened?"

"That asshole Hoar jumped out the window," Ponzie said. "We gotta get outta here before he calls the law."

"Ya think he will?" Georgie said. "He's probably wanted for something."

"Can't take the chance. We're going." Ponzie turned to me. "All right, Marlowe. You stay away from my store *and* my wife unless you want us to come back for another visit."

Ponzie headed for the door, turned back to me. "Keep your mouth shut with the cops, too. It's your word against ours. And I know a few things about you that you wouldn't want the cops or that girl of yours to know."

He snickered, shoved the gun in his waistband, pulled the sweatshirt over it, and left by the front door. Georgie the Ape followed him out.

Shamrock, Derwood, and I didn't move a muscle until we were sure they were well gone. Then Shamrock got up, closed and deadbolted the door, and headed for the kitchen. I stood, walked over to the window, and leaned out, looking to see if Eddie was about.

The only sign of Eddie Hoar was the screen down in the sand. I returned to my chair.

"He ain't there, Dan," Derwood said. "He's long gone by now. Eddie's a fast runner."

"I'm sure he is," I said.

"Yeah, you shoulda seen the time we hit the laundromat down on Ashworth. The cops are tryin' to come in the locked front door and we're going out the back. Eddie musta had fifty pounds a quarters stuffed in his pockets and he still moved like a greyhound. Right over fences, too, like it was nothin'. We had our car parked a couple a side streets over and—"

"Later, Derwood," I interrupted. I usually got a chuckle whenever I heard a story concerning the bumbling beach rip-offs but not tonight. I may have come close to getting killed. We all might have, for god's sake.

Shamrock came back into the room with three bottles of open Heineken and passed them out. His hands were shaking.

"That was a close one, Danny," he said. He put his bottle of beer up to his mouth and nearly killed it in one shot. His Adam's apple slid up and down as he swallowed.

"Eddie saved our lives," Derwood said.

Shamrock choked on his beer. "Bullshit! He was just saving his own worthless arse." He walked back to the sofa, sat next to Derwood.

I silently agreed with them both. Eddie may have unintentionally saved our lives—if Ponzie had really meant to kill us. I knew Eddie well, though. He hadn't cared about the safety of any person in this world except himself when he went sailing through that window.

"You think they woulda really killed us, Danny?" Shamrock asked.

I started to answer, "I don't know but—" and that's as far as I got.

The anxiety had been delayed as it sometimes was. The symptoms hadn't appeared during the action. But now, when my mind had plenty of time to think about what had just happened, it put in an appearance. My voice cracked, my heart raced. There was no way I could just sit. I got up from my chair almost as fast as Eddie during his diving exhibition and headed for my bedroom.

I felt Shamrock's eyes on me, but he didn't say a thing. He knew the score, after all.

The pills were still in my drawer. Either Georgie hadn't found them or tranquilizers weren't his thing. I let two dissolve under my tongue, wincing at the familiar medicinal taste. While I waited for the pills to kick in, I checked under my bed to make sure Betsy—my shotgun—was still in place. Also checked to make sure that my .38 was in my nightstand drawer. Neither weapon had been disturbed.

It doesn't take long for a drug that can be dissolved under the tongue to work, and within no time, my heart was slowing. Not to normal but to manageable.

I returned to the living room. Before I sat, I palmed one Xanax to Shamrock. He glanced at it, tossed it into his mouth, and took a sip of beer. Shamrock rarely took one of these. His relaxation method of choice was beer. I'd had a feeling, though, that tonight might be different. It's not every night that you come so close to death. Apparently, I'd been right.

When I thought I could speak again without stuttering, I did. There was something I'd remembered while I'd been waiting for the anxiety attack to subside.

"Why did you and Eddie come here anyway, Derwood?"

Derwood looked downward. "Ahh . . . I don't know."

"Come on. Tell us," Shamrock said in a reasonable tone, a tone he rarely used with the big man's partner. Shamrock hated Eddie but could tolerate Derwood. Shamrock could break Eddie in two like a stick; I was doubtful he could do the same with Derwood. We'd both seen Derwood in action before. He was not only big, he could handle himself.

Derwood looked up. "I didn't want to do it, Dan. I told him no. But you know Eddie. When he gets one of his money-making ideas, you can't stop him."

Yes, I did know that. Only too well. "What was it this time, Derwood?"

The big man looked embarrassed. "He had some information he wanted to sell you."

"Information? *Sell?*" I asked.

Derwood nodded. "Yeah. He said you'd give him two hundred for it and he'd give me half. I didn't even want the money, Dan. Besides I knew he was probably going to ask you in private for three hundred."

I knew Derwood was right on that score, but I was more interested in what the information was.

"I don't know, Dan. He wouldn't tell me. Honest. Sometimes he don't even trust me. Eddie's funny that way."

Sure, Eddie was a regular barrel of monkeys. But as far as not trusting Derwood and keeping him in the dark, I believed the big man. When you're convinced life is just one big rip-off and everyone's a potential mark, well, people like that naturally start to think everyone feels that way. I didn't doubt Eddie did.

"What the hell could that arsehole know that you'd pay the likes of him for?" Shamrock asked.

I had no idea and told him so.

"Well then," Shamrock said, looking back at Derwood. "Who was that Ponzie character and who was the hard-on he had with him?"

"He owns Seacoast Hawk Shop," Derwood said. "The place we were at. He and his wife. That's how he knew Eddie. We told you Eddie's a good customer. And that was his muscle, Georgie, with him."

I harrumphed. "Yeah, so good a customer Ponzie almost ripped his neck off with the chain."

Derwood's face reddened.

"Selma's his wife?" I asked.

Derwood nodded.

So, the hardcase woman I'd dealt with behind the counter, Selma, was married to my recent visitor, Ponzie. They made a lovely couple.

But I had some big questions: had Ponzie really intended to kill us or had he been bluffing? And why? What was he trying to do? Cover up the murder of Sal Mariani or protect the pawnshop, an obvious front for stolen goods?

Could have been either, I realized. I was only interested if his actions were related to Sal's murder, though. After all, erasing me and Shamrock from that suspect list was my goal. A small-time stolen goods operation? I couldn't have cared less.

There was one other thing tickling at the back of my mind. The man I'd seen entering the back door of the pawnshop—a man I couldn't identify although I'd seen him somewhere before. But where, for the life of me, had it been?

Chapter 16

I KNEW IT was dangerous, but I decided to try calling on Sal Mariani's girlfriend again. Sure, she might scream her fool head off and call the cops, but I was already in deep shit and I didn't think it could get much worse. At least I hoped it couldn't.

The next day I went to pay her a visit on the way to my High Tide shift. I didn't tell Shamrock. His fiery Irish temper might cause a problem. Even more than it had the first time we'd met the woman.

I made the short walk myself, and it wasn't long before I stood on the decrepit porch, rapping my knuckles on the old wooden door. It took quite a few knocks and a couple of minutes before there was any response. Finally, the door opened.

Except for appearing more worried, she looked the same as the last time I'd seen her. Maybe better. She wore a long-sleeve white top that exposed her firm midriff. The top advertised some rock group I was unfamiliar with. Her feet were bare. Her blonde hair hung in her face, partially blocking one eye. She was the best-looking junkie I'd ever seen, though the drugs would change that in time.

"You," she said. Her voice was throaty. "What are you doin' here?"

She looked nervously past my shoulders as if she expected someone to be hiding behind me. Shamrock?

"It's Dan and I just want to talk." I'd barely gotten that much out when she grabbed my arm and pulled me into the room. She slammed the door behind me and flipped a deadbolt.

"Why did you come here?" she asked. "Are you trying to get me killed?"

The look in her eyes told me she was truly terrified about something. Either that or very high.

She ran to the front window, pulled back a corner of the shade and peered out. "Were you followed? Did you bring anyone with you?"

She dropped the shade and turned to me.

I didn't have any idea what I'd just dropped into, but I played along. "No, I wasn't followed. And no, I didn't bring anyone."

She came so close I could actually feel her breasts trembling. "You could get me killed."

I decided not to let the surprise reception derail me. I cleared my throat and pulled back. "I wanted to ask you some questions about Sal."

She dashed over to a sofa that looked like it should have been stuck out front for Heavy Pickup Day. "Sal? He's dead. Forget about him. You killed him anyway."

"I didn't kill him, and you know that." From what I'd seen in the past couple of minutes, I believed that statement. She was deathly afraid of someone. If it had been me—if she thought I'd killed Sal—she wouldn't have dragged me in and locked the door.

She fidgeted nervously on the sofa. "The cops say you did."

She didn't ask me to sit. I didn't care to anyway. "You know better."

"I don't know anything and I don't want to know."

"Who really killed Sal?" I asked.

"I don't know." She tried to make the words sound believable with that slow throaty voice. But they were more distracting than believable.

"Who are you afraid of?"

Her eye twitched. "I'm not afraid of anyone."

I walked to the window, pulled up the shade.

She was out of her seat like someone had lit her ass on fire. She pulled the shade down, almost yanking it off its brackets.

"Are you crazy?" She balled her fists and for a moment, I thought she was going to take a poke at me. Fortunately, she didn't, saving us both some embarrassment.

She looked from me to the window and back again. "Okay," she said. "I'll talk to you. A little." She scowled and added, "But you can't tell anyone you've been here."

I nodded as she took her seat on the sofa. I looked down at her.

"Who killed Sal?" I asked again.

"You." She folded her arms across her stomach. She wore no bra and didn't need one.

I pushed the visual out of my mind. "Like I said, you know that's not true."

She pursed her full lips before she spoke. "Well, you might as well have. He died because of you."

"Me? Why me?"

"Because you were nosing around."

"Because of the hot jewelry? That's why he was killed?"

"I'm not saying anything else."

"You know Ponzie and Selma over at the Salisbury pawnshop?"

Her tongue came out and moistened her lips.

"I don't know anything . . ." she said in that throaty voice. She hesitated, then added, "Unless maybe you have a little something."

She looked at me, her blonde hair half-shielding one blue eye. "I need something, Dan. I'm scared."

I knew what she meant. Her shirt was long-sleeved but that didn't help hide her condition. "I don't have anything."

Then I remembered that I'd brought my vial. My increased anxiety had worried me. "A couple Xanax maybe. It'll help with being scared at least."

She snorted. "I'll take them. But that isn't going to get you many answers. You know what I need. Please, Dan. I have to keep it together for my daughter, Amy."

I was just about to say I wasn't interested in that kind of exchange when someone spoke from a doorway to my right.

"Mama, when are we gonna eat?" It was a child—a girl. Four or five, maybe. She wore pajamas and looked like Tammy must have at that age. She had long blonde hair and held a worn teddy bear clasped to her side.

Tammy spun to face her. "I'll get it as soon as I can, Amy. Can't you see I have company?"

The child lowered her head and looked at the floor, but she didn't leave.

I didn't think I was going to get any more info today. Besides, I'd lost my taste for interrogation the second the child had spoken. I turned, hiding my hands from both of them. I retrieved two pills from the vial before returning it to my pocket. I cupped the pills, stepped to the beat-up coffee table, and set them down. The child was still staring at the floor.

"Thank you, Dan," Tammy said. She scooped the pills up and dry-swallowed both.

I watched; the child didn't.

"Where's Sal's truck?" I asked, remembering I hadn't seen it in the driveway, just the older car.

"The police took it," Tammy answered.

I had nothing else to say; at least not with the little girl here. I turned for the door. "If you want to tell me anything, you know where I work."

"Please, Dan," Tammy said, her throaty voice almost a whisper now. "If you get me what I really need, I'll tell you everything I know."

With her looks, Tammy had more than likely rarely, if ever, been refused her request. "What about blow?" I said softly.

She looked surprised. "That'll be okay. But I'd rather get my regular."

I don't know why I even inquired about her preference. I had no intention of getting her drugs in exchange for information.

On the way to the High Tide, I wondered if I was as dead set against that swap as I had first thought. Things didn't seem so iron-clad with a murder rap hanging over my head.

But there was more to it than that. A lot more. My grumbling bowels told me that.

Chapter 17

"THE LIEUTENANT WANTS to see you down at the station, Mr. Marlowe."

A day later I was talking to two of Hampton's finest. The pair stood on my front porch, hands on their duty belts. It was about nine in the morning, and the knock at my front door had beaten my alarm clock by only minutes. I'd thrown on a pair of jeans to go along with the navy T-shirt I'd slept in.

"Again?" I asked. "Can I take a shower first?"

They both nodded.

"Come on in and wait if you want." I opened the screen door and held it for them as they trooped in. They took seats opposite each other. One in *my* chair, the other on the sofa. Even though I had a general idea, I still had to ask, "What's this all about?"

The older of the two, a gray-haired man with a pot belly he'd obviously worked on expanding for years, answered. "The lieutenant will tell you about it."

"It's got to be about Sal Mariani," I said, looking down at them. I waited a beat, then added, "I don't have to go if I don't want to, you know."

The older cop just shrugged.

I walked over to the TV, turned it on, and searched for something to amuse the two cops while they waited. Was it advisable to talk to Gant? I *didn't* have to, did I?

I'd heard something once about cops being able to question anyone during a murder investigation. I had no idea if that was just an old wives' tale or not. I knew one thing from experience though—the less you said to the police the better. A fool, like me, could easily incriminate himself.

But wasn't I already incriminated? I was under investigation for murder. What else could Gant hang on me?

Still, James Connolly, my attorney, wouldn't be happy about this. He'd tell me to shut up; not to talk to the cops. He'd said those exact words to me many times before.

I was in deep shit, though, along with other people. I had to take a chance that maybe I could turn the tables on Gant. Maybe he'd slip and give me a kernel of information, something that would help us all out of this dire situation.

Finally, I found the right channel for my two guests—a rerun of the *Cops* show for the cops. I didn't even have to ask them if that's what they'd like to watch. The TV had their full attention.

After I'd done a quick shit, shower, and shave, I returned to the living room.

"Ready," I said. When that only got a grunt out of the older cop, I walked over and turned off the TV. The old cop grunted again and struggled up out of my easy chair. I hoped he hadn't farted in my cushion and didn't relish sitting in my chair later.

Especially after returning from what I assumed would be an unpleasant face-to-face with my nemesis. I'd never had a pleasant encounter with Gant. Why should this time be any different?

The two cops stepped out first onto my porch and headed down the stairs. I hesitated just before closing the door and called to them that I'd forgotten my keys, even though the key ring was in my hand. I made a quick phone call—the real reason for my imaginary lost keys—and rejoined my escorts waiting out front in the cruiser. I hopped in the backseat. The old timer was driving.

We took a leisurely ride up Ocean Boulevard. It was fairly early, but quite a few people were already out. I got more than a few glances from pedestrians trying to figure out who the criminal in the backseat of the cruiser was—a woman beater, an underage drunk, or a petty thief. We got plenty of each in the summer.

I gave a few groups of people, especially those with young kids, a hearty wave as we rolled by, almost like a visiting politician or rock star. It did me good, lightening the situation for a second or two. Even put a smile on my face.

That didn't last long though. Within minutes, we'd parked in front of the police station and paraded into the building. I was left alone in the same interrogation room I'd been in before. Even though my memory wasn't good in regards to incidents way back when, I was sure I'd been in this exact room more times than I could count.

The decor hadn't changed. Gant popped in a couple of minutes after me. He closed the door behind him, louder than necessary, and sat in the chair at the head of the long desk.

He pretended to go over some papers he'd brought with him. I didn't buy it. He was crunching the papers with both hands, probably pretending my head was between his hands, not the papers. After a long fifteen seconds, he tossed the papers on the desk, pushed his chair back so hard it almost tipped over, and walked to a set of toggles and switches on the wall. He fiddled around with them. Cameras? Mic?

I couldn't be sure, but I could see the cameras in corners near the ceiling facing the desk from different directions. Of course, everything said in the interrogation room was most likely recorded—common sense told me that.

Unless someone, like Gant, didn't want it recorded.

After his tinkering with the switches was over, Gant spun around and rushed me. I instinctively threw up my arms. He put on the brakes just as he got within a foot of me. His face was florid and he leaned in closer. "You motherfuckin' piece a shit, Marlowe. I told you to stay out of the Mariani investigation."

I lowered my arms, feeling a little embarrassed. I should have kept them up, though. It might have blocked some of Gant's spittle as he continued to rant.

It wouldn't have done anything about his breath though— it was foul. A mixture of cheap coffee, stale cigarettes, and undigested cold cuts. I wondered if he ever brushed his teeth.

I raised my hand and put my palm against his chest, gently pushing.

You would've thought I'd pulled down his pants.

Gant lowered his eyes and watched in shock as I used just enough pressure to get his troublesome hygiene habit out of my range. He seemed dumbstruck as I returned my hand to my side.

When he looked up at me, I noticed red spider lines in the whites of his eyes. I tensed, ready for anything. Finally, he let out a . . . growl, turned, retook his seat. Holding the edge of the desk with both hands, he said, "I warned you, Marlowe, not to fuck up my investigation."

I thought it best not to respond to that statement. He was under semi-control. I liked it that way.

When I didn't say anything, he released his grip on the desk, and picked up the papers again. They were badly scrunched, and he took a moment to smooth them out. "You haven't just stepped out of line *once*, Marlowe. That's all you do, for Chrissake. You've been bothering everybody."

He glanced at the papers in front of him. Why, I didn't know. He certainly didn't need them. Hampton Beach was a small village. People talk. And maybe I was under surveillance. Or others I'd visited could be. So he probably was aware of my every move.

It would have been stupid to deny his claim, so I remained silent.

"I don't want to see you anywhere near anyone involved in this case again," Gant finally continued. "*Anyone.* You got me, asshole? *Anyone.* And if I hear that you have been . . . I'm gonna . . . gonna fuckin' crucify you."

I tried to keep the anger out of my voice, but it wasn't easy.

"Crucify me?" I said incredulously. "What else can you do to me, Gant? You're trying to pin a murder on me. Something I didn't have anything to do with."

"Bullshit!" This time Gant's spittle landed harmlessly on the desk between us.

"You killed that little junkie because he ripped off your girlfriend's jewelry. There's a motive right there. And here's another motive: you had Mariani working in your gang and couldn't take the chance he might squeal on you." Gant pointed a finger at my face. "You knew we were about to take him down, and he'd roll like a bowling bowl. So you had him disposed of. You and the mick. You had to get drunk, the two of you. That's why the hit was so sloppy."

He started waving his finger furiously at me, a maniacal grin on his face. "You did it this time, Marlowe. You fucked up big time."

If it had been anyone else saying these things, I would've have called for a straitjacket for him. But this was Gant. And even though he was crazy and obsessed with me, that was normal for him. But now he was driving *me* crazy and I didn't know what to do about it.

That's probably why I finally lost control. If I kept quiet any longer, and kept it all bottled in, they'd be cinching me up in that restraining jacket instead of Gant.

"You're not going to get away with this, Gant. You've gone 'round the bend. You're out of your fuckin' mind."

His teeth were partially clenched, but he still managed to breathe out the words, "Shuddup, shithead. You're behind half the crime on *my* beach and you have been for years. You think I'm stupid? You've been lucky so far. You're not getting away with this, though."

He was still fuming, but he lowered his voice to a whisper. "Even if you *didn't* do it."

I've heard of evil grins, but the one he plastered on his face took the cake.

"Fuck you, Gant. You crazy bastard. They'll have you locked up in the state nut house way before you get me for anything."

Gant looked like he wanted to stick a pencil in my eye.

"You're gonna get it, Marlowe," he sputtered. "I'm gonna nail your fuckin' hide to the wall. I'm going to have you wearing a dress and lipstick in Concord soon. And you'll probably *like* it. You've ruined my beach, you cocksucker."

I was steaming now. "Ruined *your* beach, you crazy old lunatic. You don't own the beach, thank god. You're the one that's ruined the beach for me! You're nothing but a two-bit cop who probably falls into bed with some old cow every night after you've killed a bottle of booze. Why don't you go out and get laid? What's it been, ten years? Maybe that'll do you some good."

Not wise, I know. And it wasn't like me to mention a man's wife negatively, but how much stress can one man take all at once?

"Cow!" Gant bellowed as he came out of his chair, this time pushing it completely over. His fists balled, and he yelled loudly. "You hit me first, Marlowe."

I didn't need a translator to know that meant Gant was going to give me a beating and claim self-defense. I jumped out of my chair, knocking it over in the process. Gant swung a wide left, aiming for my face. I threw my head back out of the way. I could feel the breeze on my face as his fist flew by. I stumbled to the side, regained my balance, and raised my fists.

If I could connect with the first punch as he came in, I might stagger him. Then a kick to the balls might get me into the outer hall where I could be rescued. I didn't fight much nowadays, but I had when I was younger, and I'd never have thought of kicking an opponent in the groin. This time I did; I was in fear of losing my life.

Gant had a gun on his hip.

I had only my wits.

Gant came around the desk in a rush. Just as the door flew open.

"What the hell's going on here?"

Gant spun like he'd just been caught in bed with an underage girl. "Connolly," he said, the word coming out in a strangled croak.

I hadn't realized I was huffing and puffing already, but between those huffs and puffs, I somehow got out, "James."

My hero.

Chapter 18

MY ATTORNEY EXTRICATED me from my unpleasant encounter with Lieutenant Gant and I headed directly for the Tide. I'd barely entered the back door before Dianne shouted at me. "Dan, I want to talk to you."

I didn't like the tone of her voice. Nevertheless, I went to the open office door. "What?"

She was sitting behind her desk, hands folded under her chin, a loose white restaurant shirt the only article of clothing visible. "Not here. Get Shamrock and meet me in your office."

My *office*, aka the back booth in the bar section opposite the coffee station. I turned, went through the kitchen, into the dining room, and around the partition to the bar. Shamrock was seated at the bar near the window sipping coffee. He had a cigarette going and the *Hampton Union* was spread out on the bar in front of him.

He glanced up, smiled. "Danny boy."

I motioned for him to follow me. "Come on. Dianne wants to talk to us."

He suddenly looked very uncomfortable but I ignored the look and headed for the rear. I stopped at the coffee station and proceeded to pour two cups, one for Dianne. Shamrock slid into the booth, setting both his paper and his coffee on the table. When I finished adding sweetener and cream, I carried the coffees over, set them down on the table, and slid onto the bench across from Shamrock.

He cleared his throat. "Ahh . . . Danny, I ahh . . ."

"You didn't?"

"Believe me Danny . . . I . . ."

I rolled my eyes. "You threw me under the goddamn bus, didn't you?"

Shamrock's face turned rosier than usual. "Aye, Danny, but I didn't mean it. You know how Dianne can be. She kinda got me talking and before I knew it—"

"What the hell did you tell her?"

"I told her—"

Dianne slid onto the bench beside Shamrock.

Her green eyes bored into me. "Don't be blaming him, Dan Marlowe. He's a little worried too. And I would've found out anyway."

I looked at Shamrock for no other reason than to escape the accusatory glare of Dianne's eyes. He looked as uncomfortable as I felt.

"What the hell were you thinking?" Dianne asked. She'd lowered her voice so it couldn't be heard in the dining room where the waitresses were getting their work area ready for lunch. It didn't sound any less threatening to me, though.

"Men with guns!" Her voice was louder this time. She looked nervously toward the dining room and lowered her voice again. "I could be reading about you two in *that* this morning. On the obituary page."

She banged a fist down on Shamrock's newspaper.

I kept my trap shut.

Shamrock foolishly didn't. "It wouldn't be out in the paper that quick, Dianne."

He tried to make it come out as a joke but the joke bombed, as I knew it would.

Dianne glared at Shamrock, and her eyes narrowed. "Don't be a wisenheimer."

Shamrock moved an inch closer to the wall.

"This isn't funny," Dianne insisted.

She was right about that. Still. "It wasn't all that bad," I said. "They were just bluffing. Trying to scare us off."

"I hope they did a good job of it! I know they did with *him*." She tilted her head toward Shamrock. "But what about you?"

"It wasn't that serious, Dianne," I said.

"Don't Dianne me! If it wasn't for that loser, Eddie Hoar, diving through your window, you both might be dead right now." Her eyes, still flashing, misted.

I turned my eyes on Shamrock. He mumbled, "Sorry, Danny."

"Sorry nothing," Dianne hissed. "You've got nothing to be sorry about."

She hesitated, then, "Except maybe going along with his suicidal ideas."

I held my hands, palms up, in a conciliatory gesture. "It's all over now, honey. Nothing happened."

"Nothing happened? I wonder what your neighbors are saying about that birdbrain jumping out your window?" She didn't give me a chance to answer. "Oh, that's right. Nothing unusual at Dan Marlowe's cottage. Just an average weekday night."

"What do you want me to do?" I asked, even though I already knew the answer.

"It's not just me," she said. "It's him, too."

I turned a scowl on Shamrock. He shifted in his seat. "Well, it is getting dangerous, Danny. And we don't want to jump from the frying pan into the fire."

Now it was my turn to get a little pissed. "Into the fire! We're already in the fire. Gant is trying to hang a murder on us."

"You don't know that," Dianne shot back.

"Yes, I do and so do you two."

"No, I don't know that," Dianne said. "Shamrock?" She looked his way.

He didn't answer. How could he? He knew the truth.

She spun back to me. "You two are impossible!"

We sipped our coffees. I thought it best not to be the first to talk.

"You probably both deserved it too," Dianne finally said. "That's the worst of it. You're over in Salisbury stalking the man's wife—at her business! Are you both crazy? You're lucky you didn't get arrested." She hesitated, then, "What the hell would you do, Dan, if some guy was over here stalking me at the Tide? You'd probably go and have words with him too."

"I wouldn't threaten him with a gun."

"I'm not so sure about that. Sometimes I wonder what you're capable of. Or maybe you did some permanent damage to your brain back in the day."

I felt my face turn red. She rarely went there—unless she was extremely angry.

"I have to get some work done," she said. "If I can, what with worrying about all this. I'm not even going to ask you to stop what you're doing. You won't. Or worse, you'll lie to me!"

She slid out of the booth and stood for a moment, looking down at me. "And you want to know something? I don't even know if I care anymore."

She turned and made a beeline for the kitchen.

I suddenly felt worse than I had so far during this crazy fiasco. I hadn't thought that was possible. But it was. Any time Dianne and I were on the outs was bad for me. A dark and dangerous mood usually filled my brain until the conflict was over. I'd always made it through these black periods before but I never knew if the next one would be the last one, one way or another.

Of course, I turned my anger on my friend. "You stupid idiot."

Shamrock wouldn't look at me. "I know, Danny. I done wrong. I didn't mean to. I don't know why I told her. She got a little out of me and then she seemed so worried, I told her something else, and that led to . . . You know Dianne."

Yes, I did.

I couldn't blame Shamrock too much. Dianne could be persuasive. Not only were they good friends, they both had me in common. I think they both loved me (yes, even Shamrock, although he'd never tell me that.) Neither one would do anything to hurt me. They'd both proven that through the years, more times than I deserved.

"Forget it," I said.

"I'm sorry, Danny."

"I know you are."

"I'll still help you on this Sal the Crapper thing, you know that. I couldn't tell Dianne that, though. She would've shoved the Blarney Stone up me arse."

I smiled. "Thanks."

"I gotta go, Danny." Shamrock slid from the booth. "Talk to you later."

He headed in the same direction Dianne had taken.

I sat there alone with my thoughts. There was no chance I was going to curtail my investigation into Sal Mariani's murder. No matter that Dianne didn't believe that Gant would actually hang a murder on me. I knew he would, if he could. He'd told me so. If he did, everything good in my life would be erased, including Dianne and Shamrock, not to mention my kids. I couldn't take that chance, no matter the odds.

Fortunately, Dianne hadn't found out about my meeting with Sal's girl. Knowing I'd confronted the woman again would have made Dianne's anger worse—if that was even possible. I wasn't sure I'd tell Shamrock about the encounter, either, considering what had just transpired. Although if I didn't tell him, I'd have no one to talk to about it.

Banging on the big wooden front door brought me out of my thoughts.

Eli and Paulie.

I'd forgotten the time. I reached for the *Hampton Union* Shamrock had left behind, planning to take it to the bar and peruse the paper during my down time. Something caught my eye as I slid the paper in front of me.

Right there on the front page. On the bottom fold. A face I recognized.

Now I had another angle. Where it would lead, I didn't know.

Chapter 19

"WHAT DO YOU know about him?"

I sat at a window table at the White Cap restaurant on a side street not far from the High Tide. There was a heavy smell of fried seafood. Across from me sat a friend of mine, Steve Moore. I'd phoned him and asked for this meet. Steve was a detective with the Hampton Police, and he was dressed the part in a pale blue short-sleeved shirt, a thin blue tie darker than the shirt, and black slacks. He'd tossed his sport coat on the chair beside him.

"What do you want to know," Steve answered, "and why?"

Steve studied the front page of the *Hampton Union* that I'd placed in front of him. It was the one I'd brought from the Tide, the one with the picture of the man I recognized. Michael Ferguson, a detective with the Salisbury Police Department.

"Well," I started, "I saw him going in the back door of the pawnshop over in Salisbury."

Steve furrowed his brow as he looked up at me. "Please. Start at the beginning, will you? What the hell were you doing over there . . . and what the hell were you doing eyeballing the back door of the place?"

I felt like a stalker after Steve said that. I was about to try and explain it when a waitress came up to the table. I'd seen her before. She was as old as those hills people sometimes mention.

"Menu?"

Before I could say anything, Steve spoke up. "Nah. Just a coke."

The old waitress looked at him like she probably looked at a deadbeat.

"I'll get that right away, *officer*," she said, not attempting to hide her sarcasm.

I wasn't sure if she knew Steve, but even if she didn't, the 9mm on his hip announced his profession.

It was always like this with Steve. Waitpeople aren't too appreciative when someone takes up a table and orders no more than a cold drink. For some reason, Steve had no qualms about doing just that.

It was suppertime and I was hungry, so it was more than embarrassment that had me saying quickly, "I'll have your baked stuffed haddock."

Not as good as the Tide's, but passable.

"French fries and coleslaw too, please. And a diet coke."

You'd think I ordered pheasant-under-glass the way she beamed at me.

"Thank you, sir," she said before she scurried away.

Once she was out of sight, I went back to the topic at hand and answered Steve's question. I told him the whole story from the beginning right up until that minute. Being a Hampton cop, he already knew a lot of it. I was hoping he'd tell me how deep in the shit he thought I was.

He looked at me sadly and shook his head. "How the hell do you get yourself in these predicaments, Dan?"

I didn't think he wanted an answer, and I didn't give him one.

"I was going to give you a call but you beat me to it," he said when he realized I wasn't going to answer. "Gant's got a stick up his ass about you. Of course, knowing that we're friends, he's given the Mariani investigation to someone else."

He peered around the room, then his gaze came back to me and he lowered his voice. "A little birdie told me that he's hot-to-trot to pin this on you and Kelly. So much so that he's discouraging the boys from checking on some other leads."

I let out a deep sigh. "It's that bad, huh?"

"Yes, it is. But on the positive side, the detectives aren't stupid. They know you aren't a perfect fit for this especially with the personal animosity Gant holds for you. I've been told they're looking elsewhere anyway. No stone unturned, as they say."

I shrugged. "I guess. As long as it's not my tombstone."

Steve chuckled. "Good one, Dan."

"I didn't mean it as a joke."

Steve frowned. "I guess it isn't funny, is it?"

I wanted to get back to the reason I'd had Steve come in the first place. I pointed at the face on the newspaper again. "And him? Ferguson?"

Steve snorted. "Michael Ferguson. Mikey Ferguson. Big Mikey. A fuckin' asshole."

I was surprised to hear Steve speak that way of a fellow officer. He never had before; not even about Gant.

"What's the matter with him?" I asked.

"Where do you want me to start?"

"Come on, tell me," I said.

Steve leaned over the table toward me, lowering his voice. "You keep this quiet. I'm not fooling."

"You got my word. You know me."

"Yeah, I do." He leaned back in his chair. "Ferguson's been a real scumbag ever since he came on the force."

"How so?"

"I'll tell you a story. It goes back to when Ferguson first got on the force over in Salisbury. My cousin was in the Beach Ball bar with a couple of buddies one night. You know this part—they were drinking beer, listening to some rock band. I guess they got a little rowdy or something and someone called the cops. Anyway, one of those cops was Ferguson. My cousin might have smart-mouthed him; I wouldn't put it past him. But he didn't deserve what that bastard did to him."

"What happened?" I asked.

"After he was arrested, my cousin was walking down the cell block when Ferguson cold cocked him in the back of the head. Slammed him right into the cement wall face first. Broke his nose, teeth, and his jaw. He was a mess. All wired up. To this day, he can't breathe right."

"They didn't shit-can Ferguson?"

Steve harrumphed. "The shitball said my cousin attacked him, he shoved him away in self-defense, and he stumbled into the wall."

"And they believed that?"

"Who knows? Nothing ever came of it anyway. Doesn't hurt that he's one of the old townies over there. You know what I mean?"

Yes, I did. "Old townies" had lived in Salisbury for-ever and had a long-time lock on the local politics and businesses of any significance in town. *And* they stuck to-gether. Apparently, this cop, Ferguson, was one of them. In good standing, too.

"Do you think it's possible he's involved with any crooked goings on at the pawnshop?" I asked even though I had a good idea what the answer might be.

"Ferguson could be capable of anything, Dan. Always has been." Steve gave me a look that sent a little shiver up my spine. "If you're thinking of pursuing anything he's involved in, I'd forget about it. Like I said, he's capable of anything."

I hesitated before I said, "Even murder?"

"Don't go there, Dan. If you're thinking that Ferguson had anything to do with Mariani getting killed, you're prob-ably wrong. Sure, he's vicious and a freakin' crook, but he's not stupid. He's got too many sweet rackets going on over there to screw it up by killing a junkie."

"How do you know he's involved in rackets?"

"I've heard the stories through the years. Even the state cops have poked around over there before, but they couldn't get anywhere. The lips over there are as tight as clams."

"But if a murder was involved, they'd come in harder, wouldn't they?"

The waitress came back and dropped off our drinks. She gave Steve a frown, but smiled when she turned to me and said, "Your meal'll be right up." Then she left.

Steve shook his head, looked at me with pity in his eyes. "Look, Dan, I know you're trying to get out from under this Mariani thing, but don't worry. Gant's not going to be able to pin it on you. People know your history with the man. They also know that you're no murderer. Just sit back for a while, let the detectives do their work, and it'll die a natural death. The real murderer will turn up, and Gant'll have to acknowledge it."

"I can't wait, Steve. Everybody on the beach knows about me and Shamrock getting hauled in. I'm sure the seaweed telephone line has been burning up about it. And if things go on too long, the local citizenry will have me tried and convicted. I can't have that kind of talk getting back to my ex-wife if I want to keep seeing my kids."

Steve and I were old friends, and he knew my background.

"Still, I think you're barking up the wrong tree," Steve said.

"It's the only tree I got."

"Wasting your time. The pawnshop? Stolen goods? Sure. Ferguson slipping in the back door every week to get a few bucks to ignore what they got going on? Sure, I can see that. But murder? No."

I hated to ask, but I felt I had to. "Could you help me, Steve? You know, nothing big, and only if I need it."

There was no way he'd turn me down. You see, I did him a good turn once, the kind of deed that Buddhists would say guaranteed me a good life in my next reincarnation. Too bad I wasn't a Buddhist.

He sighed long and deep. "Within reason. I've wanted to see that piece of shit go down ever since he screwed up my cousin."

He pointed a finger at me. "But I'm telling you, Dan. Keep my name out of it. This guy's a cop in a neighboring town, and he probably has friends here in Hampton. If Gant or the chief ever get wind I've helped you with whatever it is that you're going to do, my ass is grass."

He gave me a stern look. "I got a family, Dan. You know that."

Yes, I did. Steve had a beautiful family. A wonderful wife and an adopted son, Kelsey. "I'd never do anything to hurt you, Steve. And besides, I'm just going to do a little more poking around."

Steve blew out a puff of air. "I know where your poking around can end up."

I was just about to respond when the old waitress returned and set my meal in front of me. I spent the next fifteen minutes demolishing it. Except the french fries. I only had one of those. Steve had the rest.

Chapter 20

I WAS BEHIND the bar at the Tide. I'd just gotten off the phone with a mobile glass repair company and told them to stop by the cottage and fix the shattered glass in my Chevette. Except for my run-in with Gant and my meeting with Steve Moore, both the previous day, nothing else of importance had occurred. I had a couple of small ideas as to how I should proceed in finding out more about Sal Mariani's murder but nothing that really lit me on fire. I was grateful Steve had agreed to have my back and help where he could. Within reason, he'd said. I was determined to keep any request I made of Steve within those parameters. He was my friend, and I'd given him my word.

I was just winding down my shift when in came Eddie Hoar of all people. Right behind him was, of course, Derwood Doller. I wasn't happy to see Eddie. Nothing to do with the new screen I'd had to buy for my window—he was just that kind of person. Still, like it or not, sometimes we *all* have to see that kind of person.

Eddie and Derwood took seats at the bar, and I stepped over to them. Eddie's face was scratched up.

"Dan, the man," Eddie said. "How ya been?"

"Good except for the thirty bucks I had to shell out for the screen you ruined."

Eddie straightened his shoulders. "Screen? You're complainin' about a screen? Look at my face, man. I'm worried I might have scarring."

I studied Eddie's face. He was exaggerating, of course. The scratches barely broke the surface of his skin and were already healing. Anyway, with Eddie's pockmarked face, a few small scars might have done his appearance some good.

"Besides," Eddie began, suddenly sounding as proud as a Marine. "I saved your life."

That was an awful thought, and I couldn't let Eddie assume I owed him that type of obligation. It could haunt me for years, and I knew it. "Eddie, you dived out that window to save your own skin. You didn't give a shit what happened to the rest of us."

"Told ya that Dan was wise to ya, Eddie." Derwood had a big smirk on his face. He turned toward me. "He wouldn't have even cared if I got shot, Dan, and I'm Eddie's best friend."

Eddie looked sullen. "Shuddup, Dumwood."

Derwood took Eddie by the front of his shirt, shook him forcefully. "I told you not to call me that, Eddie. I hate it."

He let go of the shirt and balled his fist. Eddie threw his hands up protectively.

I had no idea whether Derwood would pop Eddie in my place of work or not, but I didn't want to find out. Besides, I'd seen this comedy routine many times before and I was sick of it. I reached across the bar, grabbed Derwood's fist. "Knock it off, you two. This is a business."

Derwood relaxed his fist. Eddie, seeing that he wasn't going to get punched in the nose, acted indignant as he smoothed the wrinkles in his shirt.

I don't know why he bothered. Derwood's scrunching hadn't made it appear any worse. When he first walked in, the shirt had already looked like Eddie'd slept in it.

"I was only kidding," Eddie said. "You gotta lighten up, Derwood."

"What do you want, Eddie?" I said, hoping it wasn't much. "Menu? Drink?"

"Nah, nah, nah," Eddie said, shaking his head and thumbing his chest at the same time. "I got important business to discuss with you."

Important business? I'd almost forgotten about the info that had supposedly brought Derwood and Eddie to my cottage that night.

The info Eddie wanted to sell me.

I had no idea what it was, but I *was* interested. You never knew after all. Besides I was desperate for anything that might clear our names—both Shamrock's and mine.

"All right," I said as my replacement came around the bar. "Meet me over there." I nodded toward my empty *office* booth near the back of the restaurant.

"Okay," Eddie said, sliding off his stool. "And bring a top-shelf cognac, will ya? And a beer for my associate."

I didn't answer. What was the point? I wanted to hear the info Eddie claimed he had, and the drinks would be all he'd get if his dope was worthless. I brought the damn top-shelf cognac for Eddie and a beer for Derwood and joined them in the booth.

"All right, Eddie, what's this hot info you got for me?"

Eddie licked his lips and said, "Hold on, Dan."

He held up the cognac glass and tipped it toward Derwood. The big man clinked the glass with his beer bottle and then Eddie turned the glass toward me. I didn't have a drink, so I shrugged and held up my empty hand, anxious to get this over with. Eddie tapped the glass lightly against my hand, moved the glass to his thin lips, and drained it in one big gulp.

He let out with a long, "Ahhh."

Then he wiggled the glass in front of my face and added, "How about another, Dan?"

"I'll buy you another when you pay for the damn screen you wrecked."

"*Well*," Eddie said, a forced look of shock on his face. "That was to save your life."

"Your life's more like it, Eddie," I said. "Now cut to the chase. What's this information you got for me?"

Eddie leaned back in the booth. "I hate to say this, Dan, but this is very top-secret information. And dangerous to *me*! I'd be risking my life. But for a good friend like you, I could let you have it for . . ." He hesitated, turned to Derwood. "Go get me a beer, will ya, Derwood?"

I knew the score, and I knew even the not-too-bright lummox seated beside Eddie knew it, too.

"I ain't payin' for it," Derwood said. "You never pay me back."

"Ungrateful," Eddie said as he pulled two crumpled ones from his pants pocket and threw them down on the table. I was sure Derwood knew that two dollars wouldn't cover even one bottle of beer, let alone a tip. Maybe Derwood thought he was getting away easy by only paying a fraction of the cost of Eddie's beer or maybe it was something else. Whatever was going on in the big man's head, Derwood gave Eddie a scowl, scooped up the bills, and headed for the bar.

When Derwood was out of earshot, Eddie said, "Keep this between you and me, will ya, Dan? You know how Dumwood is. He ain't right up here."

He tapped his head with his forefinger. "I don't want to upset him. He don't know business like you and me do."

"Cut the comedy, Eddie. I know what you mean." I remembered the figures Derwood had mentioned at my cottage. "I'll give you two hundred bucks if the information is worthwhile. Nothing if it isn't."

Eddie looked like he couldn't decide whether to be perplexed or frightened. "I don't know. I was thinkin' three hundred."

Before he could finish, I started to slide out of the booth. Eddie grabbed my wrist. "Hold on. Don't get excited. Sure, sure, two hundred's fine."

I slid back into the booth. "It better be good, Eddie, or you get nothing."

Eddie smirked but didn't say a word.

"Give or I'm leaving." I could only take so much from this guy.

"Okay, okay. Hold your horses. This is it." Eddie slowly surveyed what he could see of the room, then leaned across the table toward me and spoke in almost a whisper. "You know Seacoast Hawk Shop over in Salisbury?"

His breath was foul, and I pulled back a bit to get out of range. "Of course I know it. I went there with you, you dumb-ass."

Eddie sat back and looked at me like I was the dumb ass. "Yeah, but you don't know who they're tied in with." He thumbed his scrawny chest. "I do."

"Who?" was all I said.

With a triumphant smile on his face, Eddie said, "Mikey Ferguson. The cop."

Just then Derwood returned, plunked a bottle of our cheapest beer down in front of Eddie, and retook his seat.

I'd been almost holding my breath, hoping that Eddie would tell me something worthwhile. Something I didn't already know. Good thing I hadn't paid in advance.

It was still possible I might get something of value beyond this bit of old news.

"I already know about Ferguson, Eddie. That info's worthless to me."

Eddie's eyes bugged.

"Worthless!" he sputtered. "But, how . . . how . . . ?"

I didn't think it would hurt to tell Eddie the truth. Besides, his special skills—loathsome as they were—might still come in handy in the quest to keep me and Shamrock out of a cell in Concord State Prison.

"I scoped out the shop, Eddie. Saw Big Mikey going in the back door. I knew he wasn't going in to pawn his gold teeth. So, I asked around. Picked up some dirt and then put two and two together."

Eddie's face had turned pastier than usual, if that were possible. "But there's more. More that you don't know about."

Eddie sounded about as desperate as a man could sound. I wondered if he'd already spent the money he'd thought he was going to get from me. If he had, he probably owed it to a biker speed dealer who had fronted dope to him. I knew the biker would be none too happy to have Eddie stiff him. And Eddie knew it, too.

I didn't expect much, but still I was hopeful. "What is it, Eddie?"

There was a slight sparkle in Eddie's eyes, like he saw there was still a possibility he might avoid a motorcycle-boot ass-kicking. "Big Mikey's not shaking down just the pawnshop. He's hitting up everyone over there except the churches. He's doing strip clubs, bars, arcades, drug dealers, whores, everything."

"Whores?" I said stupidly. "I didn't know there was any of that over there."

"Ahh, don't be so naive, Dan."

Naive? Maybe I was.

I shrugged. "Well, that helps a little."

Eddie's eyes sparkled more.

"I said a little," I quickly added.

His eyes lost their luster.

"Maybe fifty bucks worth."

"Fifty bucks?" Eddie squeaked. "But . . . but Derwood and I got obligations."

Derwood had been silent since he'd returned from the bar. But not now. "I ain't got any obligations. You bought that dope, Eddie, not me. I don't even like it. And I told ya not to until you had the money in your hand."

"That's it, Dumwood, throw me under the bus," Eddie muttered.

Before Derwood could react, I jumped in. "Enough of that shit. I haven't got time for it."

I glared at Eddie. "If you want your two hundred bucks, you're going to have to work for it."

"Work?" Eddie said in a high-pitched voice. Sounded more like he'd just received a death sentence than an offer of cash.

"Yeah, that's right, Eddie," I said. "Work. You're gonna help me and Shamrock clear our names of this Sal Mariani mess."

Eddie pointed his thumb at his chest. "Me?"

"Yes, you," I said. I turned to Derwood. "And you too."

The big man looked surprised. "Why me? I didn't do nothing. I like ya, Dan, but I don't want to get mixed up in murder."

"You want to see your friend get kick-stomped by some bikers?" I asked. "Or maybe even worse? There's always room down in the marsh for another body . . . or even two."

Eddie's Adam's apple slid up and down as he croaked, "Okay, okay, we'll help you. But you'll give me the two hundred? Right?"

"I'll give it to you, Eddie," I promised.

And I would too. I couldn't have Eddie's beating or worse on my conscience. I already had enough piled up in that conscience to last a lifetime. "Derwood has to help, though."

Eddie turned to Derwood. "You're in, aren't ya, Derwood? For your best friend? Sure you're in, right?"

"Well, I don't . . . ." The big man hesitated. "Why should I help? I ain't got nothing to worry about."

I jumped in. "Sorry, Derwood, but I think you do."

"Huh?" Derwood said, looking puzzled.

"Everybody on the seacoast knows you're Eddie's partner. I'm sure whoever Eddie copped the dope from knows that. They come after him, they'll grab you too. Two hundred bucks is two hundred bucks. Doesn't matter who it comes from. They won't care."

Derwood looked at Eddie as if he were ready to tear the smaller man's head off. "You done it to me again, Eddie. I'm always getting in trouble because of you."

Then he turned to me. "You'll give us the money if we help you, Dan?"

"You got my word on it."

"Fine," Derwood said, the word dripping with resignation. "I'll help too."

He turned back to Eddie. "But not to save *you*, Eddie. To save *me*. You deserve a good beating. I might even give it to you."

Eddie was silent. He probably didn't dare disturb what seemed to be the only possible way out of his dangerous situation. Finally, he said. "What do you want us to do, Dan?" His voice was so soft I could barely hear him.

"I'm not sure yet." And I really wasn't.

I had no idea how I could use Eddie and Derwood. As a matter of fact, I had no idea what Shamrock or I could do.

But I was sure an idea would come to me. It always had. I had to hope it would again.

Before it was too late.

Chapter 21

I STARTED WITH the best of intentions like I generally did.

After my meeting with Eddie and Derwood, I left the Tide. I didn't head for my cottage, though. Instead, I banged a left down a side street and headed for Ashworth Avenue. I wasn't going to Tammy's, Shamrock's or to the police station to see Steve Moore. I was headed for a shabby little hovel on a back street off Ashworth.

Ever since Sal Mariani's girlfriend had said she had information on Sal's killer in exchange for speed, I'd grappled with the idea of getting her a little "help." At first, I rejected the notion. Not out of a sense of morality or the fear of getting caught, although I was a little troubled by both of those thoughts. No, there was something bigger bothering me. Otherwise I would have gotten the drug right away and returned to see what she had to say. After all, what she knew might get me out of a murder rap.

You see I had a drug problem not too long ago. The rich man's speed—cocaine.

I'd lost my family, the High Tide—which had been mine at the time—and my money. Not to mention my self-respect.

To say it had been bad would be an understatement. After a long hard struggle, I'd finally beaten it.

Or so I thought.

And that was the problem—I wasn't really sure I could resist the temptation to indulge if I exposed myself to the drug again.

And I'd have to if I wanted to buy whatever information Tammy had in her head.

Speed hadn't been my thing so I had no idea where to get it. Cocaine, though, was different. Tammy had agreed to accept that form of payment. And I knew exactly where to get that.

I'd once been a familiar sight at the address off Ashworth Avenue. As I walked up the rickety porch steps, my growling bowels warned me I might be lying to myself. I hoped not. Still, the left side of my brain fought with the right as I rapped on the door. It didn't take long to open.

And there he stood—my old acquaintance and coke supplier—Gil Brewer. He didn't look any different—still wore glasses, brown hair of a reasonable length, and clothes that were a step or two above what you'd expect someone living in the neighborhood to wear.

"Dan! Jesus Christ, what the hell? Come in, come in." Gil moved aside so I could enter the main room. I did, and he closed the door behind me.

The inside of the place hadn't changed either. Gil was one of those rare coke dealers that somehow could control their own intake and the inside of his house reflected that. There was a nice sofa, a couple of matching easy chairs, end tables with lamps, and an expensive stone-topped coffee table. The place was neat as a pin. The exact opposite of what you'd expect from the front of the house.

Gil never splurged on repairs and paint for the outside of the house but it wasn't because he didn't have the money. He had it. I knew that. I assumed, by what I'd picked up through the years, that when he'd first inherited this house from his grandmother and moved in, he'd decided it might not pay to overdress a house, to make it different from its neighbors. To stand out and draw attention.

And he must have been right. As far as I knew, Gil had never had any trouble with the Hampton cops, never mind state or federal. If there was more to the lack of police interest than his security precautions and luck, I had no idea. And I really didn't care. He'd never hurt me or mine in the past.

He directed me to a chair and took a seat across from me on the sofa, the stone coffee table the only thing between us.

"Are you still at the Tide?" he asked.

I smiled. "Yup, still there."

"Been meaning to come up and see you but . . ." he trailed off, looked uncomfortable, then added, "been kinda busy."

I knew he hadn't really been too busy to drop by the Tide. More likely, knowing Gil as I did, he'd been just plain thoughtful by staying away from me.

He knew my whole sordid drug story, of course, being my preferred coke dealer back in the day. You see, Gil was what you don't read or hear about concerning the "War on Drugs." He was a good drug dealer, or at least as good as one could be during a so-called war. I knew he felt guilty about my messed-up life and my losses. He knew me and he knew his product very well. Not a big leap to know even seeing him would be a temptation. That's the kind of person Gil was.

We chatted about old times for a while, Gil trying to stay away from any direct reference to the drug that had ruined my life. When he did slip, then got right off the subject, it caused a little embarrassment in both of us that only added to the nervousness I felt—the nervousness about being on a cocaine mission and the drug most likely only steps away from me.

When I couldn't wait any longer, I brought the topic up.

"I was wondering if you got anything around, Gil?" I asked my voice cracking and making me feel like a damn fool.

He looked at me with sad eyes behind his glasses.

"You're using again, Dan?" he said warily.

"No, no," I answered. "It's for a friend."

I felt stupid saying it. But what else could I say? It was the truth. I hoped.

Gil stared at me. He wore one false upper front tooth on a plate and that tooth started clicking up and down.

He had only done that when he either dipped into his own wares or was just plain nervous. Since he hadn't left the room since I'd come and had just started with the clickety-clacking, I assumed he was uncomfortable with my request.

"It really is for someone else," I said, trying to keep the shakes out of my voice and not sure if I succeeded or not.

"Yeah, I got some," he said finally. Usually this was the point where, in the past, Gil would wax eloquently on the virtues and high quality of what he had. Instead he got up and shuffled to his bedroom like a down-on-his luck hobo.

Before he could get out of sight, I said, "How about an eight-ball?" I needed the large amount, three-and-a-half grams, in case Tammy held out for more, or so I told myself.

He turned and gazed at me, nodding sadly

"Could you make one a two-gram and the other a one-and-a-half?" I got the words out somehow.

He looked puzzled. "You dealing?"

I shook my head. "No, of course not. That's just what my friend wanted."

For the next five minutes I sat perspiring in the fairly cool room, perusing a lot of nothing—knickknacks and what not. When Gil finally returned, he handed me a plastic ziplock bag with two tied-off corner baggies inside. I shoved them in the pocket of my walking shorts and pulled out my wallet.

"What do I owe you, Gil?"

"Two seventy-five'll be fine." He didn't sound happy.

I stood up as I handed him the money. This investigation was getting expensive, but right now, I didn't care. Although I liked Gil, my heart had started to race, and I wanted to get out of there.

"I guess I might as well take off now," I said.

He offered his hand. I hoped he wouldn't feel how clammy mine was.

If he did, he didn't mention it. "Nice seeing you, Dan."

Then he looked at me searchingly, and I noticed his tooth had stopped clickety-clacking. "Be careful," he said.

I left the house, went up the street to Ashworth, and turned in the direction of Tammy's home. Unfortunately, I didn't make it. Deep down, I'd known I wouldn't.

Chapter 22

COCAINE IS A funny drug. Not ha-ha funny. More like doing-your-taxes-while-trying-to-hide-income funny. It's a very serious business. At least for me. Only a person who sees . . . no . . . *feels* that type of seriousness regarding coke—or some other substance—knows what I mean. Since the minute I'd left Gil's house the cocaine was all I could think about. Reason went out the window.

It was still light out when I got to my house. I closed and locked the door behind me. Then I pulled the shades. With the shades drawn and the light on, it might as well have been night. I didn't have to show up at the Tide tomorrow, so I had a nice cushion of time. Or so I told myself. With cocaine, time moves at hyper speed, and no matter how much time I had clear on my slate, it probably wouldn't be enough.

But I didn't care about that. I dumped out some of the product on my bedroom bureau. There was a nice sparkly rock in the mix, and I went at it with my driver's license— chop, chop, chop. Laid out two long, thick lines. Took out my wallet and rolled a dollar bill. I took the lines up my pipes like I still did it all the time.

And that's when my world changed. Not a pleasant change; it was anything but. My heart sped up and I found myself drawn to the kitchen and my refrigerator like I was metal and there was a giant magnet there. The magnet was beer and lots of it. I was well stocked before I started this little trip. Otherwise I would have made a pitstop at Patriot's Corner Grocery on the way home. I pulled two beers from the fridge, popped the caps, and went back into the living room. I was barely in my easy chair before I'd drained half of one bottle.

Paranoia crept into my brain and I was nailed to my chair.

Why would a person do cocaine when they knew this would be the outcome and possibly a lot worse? Some of the experiences I had way back during the beginning of my drug use—the "Cocaine Honeymoon" period—were so pleasurable, so fun, that after the honeymoon had died—no matter how many times I tried to replicate it and failed—I'd continue to try again and again.

You know that old saying "What's madness? Trying the same thing over and over with the same negative results." Or the W. C. Fields' piece of show business advice: "Try, try and try again; but don't be a damn fool about it."

I guess it might be that way with every substance of abuse for every substance abuser. Most people learn you only have one drug honeymoon, never two, or three, or four. One. Period. I thought I'd learned that a while back. I guess I hadn't.

Against everything you'd think a sane person would do, when I could finally get out of the chair I returned to the bedroom.

To do more blow.

The thoughts that enter a drug user's mind differ depending on the person and the state of their addiction. Whatever form, they always focus on one main theme. Mine appeared only moments after the first sniff, but I couldn't act on them. Couldn't act on anything besides the next hit. The paranoia was that great.

I opened the top drawer on my bureau and rummaged around under the socks. Found the prescription vial, pulled it out, and opened it.

One pill tumbled out.

I was shocked. I'd been so focused on getting home with the coke and knowing I had plenty of beer, I'd forgotten to check my Xanax before I indulged to see if I had enough to get me through whatever coke run was going to take place. With the better part of an eight-ball left, minus a few lines, it was going to take a lot more than the one little 5mg pill to get me through the night.

I let most of the pill dissolve under my tongue, then returned to my chair.

To say the beer and the single pill could keep the paranoia away would have been a lie. Except for trips to the kitchen for more beer, to the bedroom for more lines, and once or twice to change the channel on the television, that was the extent of my physical movements. I didn't even dare go to the john for a piss. There was danger everywhere. I could hear it outside my windows—someone moving, trying to peek in. I knew it was foolish, but to me—at that time and loaded to the gills—the sounds and noises of danger were as real as the words in front of you.

In the past, even after my *Honeymoon* phase had long ended but fortified by booze and tranquilizers, I'd made the trip up to the strip and hit every watering hole on the beach. Sometimes that's all it was—a mad dash from bar to bar, looking for something, never finding it, and ending up back in my cottage after there was no business left open. Sometimes, though, the night would include unpleasant events. Some I've mentioned before; some I'll never speak about.

There was one good thing about this phase of falling off the cocaine wagon with the accompanying paranoia—I wasn't leaving this cottage unless I was forced to by someone with a gun to my head. I was afraid to go to the bathroom, for god's sake.

Such was the state I was in when I heard footsteps coming up my front stairs for the umpteenth time tonight. There was something different about the sounds of these feet. Something that told me they weren't part of my coke horrors. I glanced at the ship's clock on my wall.

Almost one-thirty a.m. Time is not a friend when I'm using cocaine. Not even close.

The booming feet on my steps stopped, my screen door creaked, and then someone tapped lightly on the door. It was no hallucination. It was real. My heart banged against my chest, and I tried to hold my breath, but instead it rushed out fast and hard. If I didn't move, maybe whoever it was would go away.

If they didn't, I'd sit here until doomsday.

I didn't get the chance because the next thing I knew, there was a scratching at the keyhole, and I watched in horror as the knob turned and the door opened and in came . . . Shamrock!

My heart didn't slow like you'd think it would. Even though this was my best friend and I had nothing to fear I was still caught up in paranoid delusions.

Sure, I'd known that Shamrock had a key. Since the fire at his place he'd been staying here off and on when he wasn't staying with one of his Irish friends. But I'd had some crazy notion that I'd be sound asleep by the time he came home, if he did. He stood there not saying a word. Just looked at me, kind of embarrassed. I was clutching the sides of the chair like I was on a roller coaster. I can imagine how my eyes looked, and as wired as I was, my jaw probably was going a mile a minute. The air conditioner I'd turned up high had the place as cold as a meat locker.

"You okay?" was all my friend said.

I tried to smile, but my face must have looked like a grotesque mask. I couldn't fool Shamrock and I knew it. "No."

Shamrock scoped out the room. There were empty beer bottles strewn about.

"You want another beer?" He must have noticed that there was only an empty on the end table beside me. I'd been too paranoid to go to the kitchen and get one. The last time I moved had been when I'd finally dashed to the bathroom before my bladder exploded. I didn't remember when that was, either.

Shamrock passed by me and returned with three open Heinekens. He placed two on my end table and took the other with him to the couch. I grabbed one with trembling hands that I hoped Shamrock couldn't see. I don't know why I cared at this point. I knew I was a mess. And he'd seen it all before anyway. I chugged the cold beer down. Then I hung onto the bottle like it was a club as my eyes darted around the room, afraid to land anywhere.

"How about your pills . . . or maybe two, Danny?" Shamrock said. The concern on his face was like a blinking neon sign.

"None left," I said with a shaky voice that embarrassed me even in my condition.

"Let me double-check," he said, getting up and heading for the bedroom before I could stop him.

I heard him rummaging around which didn't slow the perspiration oozing from my pores any. When he came out, he gave me a look—part amazement, part worry, part anger.

"You finished the whole eight-ball? Three-and-a-half freakin' grams?"

I didn't say anything. I couldn't speak without my voice shaking. Anyway, what could I say? He knew the score.

He didn't sit. "I don't like this, Danny. I'm going to take your keys and get you something. You're wired, man. And I'm nervous."

I just nodded.

After he retrieved my car keys from the key holder in the kitchen, he opened the door. He looked at me hard. "You leave here, I'll beat your fuckin' ass."

I shook my head. I couldn't have left, even if I wanted to. I was lucky if I could get out of the chair. Shamrock probably knew all that. After he was gone, I waited. It was the longest half-hour in my life.

Chapter 23

SHAMROCK RETURNED WITH a generous supply of Valium. It brought me down so I could finally sleep. I lost a day, but it could have been worse. A lot worse. Still, there were a lot of negatives. Besides the monumental crash with accompanying depression, I suffered a ton of guilt. Experience told me the guilt would take around two weeks to wear off.

And it would never disappear completely.

Even worse—Shamrock had copped the Valium from Dianne. I'd known it the minute he'd come back so quickly. She had a prescription for the drug that she rarely used except when business in the summer was at its hair-raising worst.

I couldn't blame him for going to her. When he'd realized I'd done the entire eight-ball, he was worried that I'd OD.

I knew better, of course. If I'd been going to OD, it would've happened as soon as I'd taken the last hit. But Shamrock couldn't know that. He'd never done the amount I had.

Shamrock told me he'd known what to expect. Gil Brewer, my coke dealer, had tracked him down at the

Crooked Shillelagh and told him he was worried about me. Even the coke dealer had been trying to help.

I couldn't blame Gil. Couldn't blame Shamrock. There was only one person to blame—me.

As I said, I'd be toting guilt the size of a boulder on my shoulder for about two weeks before the guilt shrank to the size of a large rock. Eventually to a stone and then maybe even someday, a pebble. How long that entire process took for me, or anyone else, I had no idea. I hadn't reached that stage yet.

And if that wasn't bad enough, a bad coke crash—or maybe a crash from any stimulant—also made a person lose their confidence. It didn't start to come back for about—you guessed it—two weeks.

I didn't have two weeks.

I wasn't sure I even had two days before Gant showed up with an arrest warrant for murder with my name on it.

The morning I was supposed to return to work started with guilt and insecurity and a phone call. Dianne was so pissed off, she told me not to come in and not to come back, *period*. She then hung up the phone.

Had I really been fired from the bar I'd once owned? For good? Maybe not. This had happened before, but the last time had been so long ago, I couldn't decide if she was madder this time. How the hell could I blame her?

I decided to stay clear of her—and the Tide. For a while anyway. At least, I wouldn't have to face the embarrassment of seeing her.

I decided to take a walk on the beach, toward the jetty. Even though it was a hot sunny day and the beach would be mobbed, the odds of meeting anyone I knew out there on the sand were small. That's what I wanted. I felt like talking to someone I knew about as much as I wanted to testify before a Grand Jury.

I was just about ready to leave when the phone rang. It was Sal the Crapper's girlfriend, Tammy.

"I've got that information for you that you wanted."

She sounded nervous but considering how I felt, and what she was into, it didn't set off any alarm bells. "Well, I don't have what you wanted." I'd done it all myself, for Christ's sake.

"That's okay. Come down. I'll tell you anyway."

I had the confidence of a mouse. "Can't you tell me now?"

"No. Only in person."

I felt like playing private detective about as much as I felt like doing a roofing job in hundred-degree weather. A private detective, even an amateur one, needs brass balls. Mine were more like jello shots. Still, I knew I had to suck it up. I was trying to beat a murder rap, after all.

"All right," I said, even though it felt anything but all right.

I left my cottage, headed up the street toward the harbor. After I'd crossed Ocean Boulevard, I banged a right onto Ashworth Avenue. The traffic was heavy. I cut across to the other side of the street, weaving between cars. Someone blew a horn at me. I gave them the finger.

My mood had shifted to black. Another side effect of the post-bender crash. The black occasionally pushed out the guilt and self-loathing, then bounced back again.

Had to be careful when the darkness descended. I could be a downright bastard, even to people I liked or loved. I accepted these states as consequences of doing my drug of choice. I'd known they would appear before I indulged, so again, no one to blame but myself.

I didn't see anyone I knew on the walk to Tammy's house. And that was good. I would have either fled to the other side of the street when I'd seen them or gone right up to them and bit their head off for no reason. Depending on what pole my psyche was attached to at that time.

When I reached Tammy's house, I rapped on the door which was closed. Odd—seeing it was hot out and I saw no A/C units jutting from the windows.

It didn't take more than a couple of seconds before Tammy opened the door, inch by inch. When it was open wide enough so I could squeeze in, I did. The air was musty.

Someone grabbed my forearm as hard as a vise and yanked me the rest of the way into the dingy room. I stumbled, and when I regained my balance, I glanced around.

The whole gang was there. My old friend Ponzie—standing in front of me. He was wearing a white wife-beater and had a smirk on his face. Next to me stood Georgie the Ape, the guy who'd pulled me in. He looked as threatening as ever. On my other side stood Tammy. She looked so frightened; I knew they'd probably forced her to call me.

There was one more person in the room—a man seated on a ratty dark barrel chair directly in front of me.

Sergeant Mikey Ferguson of the Salisbury Police.

He was as ugly as his newspaper picture. There was a big black mole on his cheek. He wore a cheap suit that strained to cover his fat body. No tie and a wrinkled white dress shirt with a collar that needed cleaning. A very ugly man. I wondered if that was why he needed extra dough. He certainly couldn't buy much with a face and body like that.

"So you're Dan Marlowe," Ferguson said.

I said nothing; I didn't think it was a question. But Georgie said something with his foot when he kicked me hard in the shin. I groaned, almost went down. My eyes teared.

Ferguson said, "Be a big boy, Marlowe. Shake it off."

He lolled his tongue around the inside of his mouth. "You're one nosy motherfucker. Why are you like that, huh?"

I answered quickly this time, before Georgie had time to attack. "I'm trying to get myself out of some trouble."

Ferguson grunted. "You? Trouble? From what I know, Trouble's your middle name."

This time I was sure there wasn't a question there. I glanced at Georgie out of the corner of my eye hoping he felt the same. Apparently, he did.

Ferguson rested his hands on the arms of the chair as he spoke. There were little flecks of white at the corners of his mouth. "I don't care about your troubles one fuckin' bit. What I do care about is you're causing *me* trouble."

He glanced at Tammy standing beside me. "And it's got nothing to do with her junkie boyfriend. I got no idea what the hell happened to him."

He turned back toward me and leaned forward in the chair. "What I do know is that you're disturbing some mighty important people around here. Business people. Big business people. And they don't like it. And neither do I, Marlowe. Get it?"

I didn't speak. I was still wary of the Ape, but luckily he didn't move.

Ferguson pinned me with those tiny black eyes. "We been good to you and that Irish friend of yours. Tried to be reasonable. Gave you a couple of warnings."

He shook his ugly head. "You didn't take 'em. We're gonna have to get a little more persuasive, I think."

Just then Tammy's young daughter, Amy, came into the room. A small blue blanket hung from her hand and dragged on the floor. It looked like it had been chewed on by a family of starving rats.

"Momma, when are we gonna eat?" she said in a voice barely above a whisper.

Tammy spun toward her, took two quick steps and said, "Now, honey. We're gonna eat right now."

"No one's eating anything," Ferguson snarled.

Tammy turned, terror in her eyes. Her daughter took a few small steps back.

"But I gotta feed my little girl," she whimpered.

"Shuddup," Ferguson said, "or I'll slap the little brat around."

Tammy disintegrated before my eyes. She began wailing and crying hysterically so loud I was sure the neighbors would hear.

Ferguson must have thought the same. He looked alarmed and called to the Ape. "All right, Georgie. Give the kid a whack. We'll see if her mother shuts her trap then."

Georgie turned and moved toward Tammy's daughter. I was scared, but I didn't feel depressed or insecure like I had back at my cottage. I'd left those feelings on the other side of the door. Now I felt fear—for the little girl.

Georgie grabbed the terrified girl's arm and raised his other hand with an open palm. I made a quick decision. I wanted to live, sure, but if I couldn't look at myself in the mirror the next day, what good was living?

I sprang across the room in three steps and caught Georgie with my left fist on the back of his head, behind his ear. I put everything I had behind the punch, but still I was amazed when the Ape went down like I'd tagged him with a crowbar. He moaned and writhed on floor.

Tammy's daughter screamed. Her mother had been shocked silent. So, surprisingly, had Ferguson and Ponzie who looked like they couldn't believe what they'd just seen. But they were only shocked senseless for a moment.

Ponzie made the first move.

"You no good fuckin' son of a bitch," he growled and came toward me. Behind him, I got a quick peek at Ferguson struggling to get out of his chair, fumbling with his suit coat as he did. I grabbed a lamp off a table and swung at Ponzie. My luck was running hot and it held. The lamp connected with his head and he stumbled and fell, clutching his face.

I spun toward Ferguson, but I was too late. The big cop was out of his chair, his police automatic pointed directly at my gut. He was sweating and had a crazy look in his eye. "It ain't gonna work, trying to scare you, Marlowe. I'm going to just do you here. Make it look like police business."

I had no idea how he hoped to get away with killing me here. Unless he was bluffing like his friend Ponzie may have been back at my cottage. But he sure didn't look like he was bluffing.

I didn't stand a chance—gun against a busted-up table lamp. But just as I decided to make a suicide rush at Ferguson, there was movement off to one side.

Tammy.

I'd almost forgotten about her. I guess Ferguson must've too because he looked as surprised as I felt when Tammy barreled into his bulky body, knocking him sideways. His gun went off as he tried to regain his balance.

"You shot me! You shot me!"

It all happened so fast, I wondered for a moment if I was the one screaming.

But it wasn't me.

Ponzie scrambled off the floor, a hole in his left shoulder—a through-and-through—dying his wife-beater bright red.

Ferguson smacked Tammy out of the way. Took one look at Ponzie holding his shoulder, blood pouring from between his fingers, then turned the gun back on me.

"You!" he hissed.

Your mind works fast when it's the only thing between you and death.

"You can't shoot us now, Ferguson," I said. "You're going to have to take your man here to the hospital. They'd put two and two together, know Ponzie was involved. That would bring it awful close to you."

I took a breath and turned to Ponzie.

"Better get to the hospital, Ponzie," I continued, not waiting for Ferguson to comment. The less time he had to think this through, the better. "You're bleeding to death."

"Jesus," Ponzie said. He glared at Ferguson. "You gotta take me to the emergency room. I'm losing a lot of blood."

I knew Ferguson wouldn't kill me now. He had too much to lose, what with all those shake-down rackets he had over in his hometown and the dough he made from them. He liked money too much to risk losing it by killing me under these circumstances.

He put the gun back in his shoulder harness under his sport coat. Told Ponzie to go and get in the car.

"And don't bleed on my upholstery," he added as Ponzie took an old coat off a wall rack, threw it over his bad shoulder and went out the door.

Georgie rose groggily to his feet. I still couldn't believe the damage I'd done with one blow, especially to a gorilla like that. Knowledge to tuck away for the future.

"Get out in the car," Ferguson ordered him.

Georgie shook his head as if trying to clear it, walking past me without even looking. Somehow, he seemed a lot smaller.

Ferguson scowled. "Don't forget what I told you, Marlowe. Butt out. If either of you mention this to anyone, I'll come back for all three of you."

He stormed out.

Tammy, who'd been silently watching, ran over to Amy, gathered her in her arms, and stroked her hair, murmuring softly to her.

I stood there like a dunce, until finally, Tammy turned toward me, set her daughter down gently on the floor. She had a red welt on her face where Ferguson had hit her. She walked over and wrapped her arms around me. I put my arms around her and held her thin body tightly. She sobbed, and I could feel her shaking.

"You . . . saved . . . Amy's . . . life."

I didn't see it that way. I'd done what I had to do for a selfish reason—so I could look at myself in the mirror. No, Tammy had saved *my* life.

I almost thanked her. But something inside told me not to mention it. I didn't know what that something was but it was speaking loud and clear.

So, I just stood there holding Tammy. Amy came up and held onto our legs. I don't know how long we stood like that. Eventually Tammy's sobs became much less frequent and her body finally stopped trembling.

Then she pulled a bit back from me and looked up into my face. "Dan, you were shaking."

And all along I thought it had been her.

Chapter 24

"TAMMY'S TERRIFIED, STEVE. She doesn't want to talk to anyone about what happened, including the cops."

I'd met Steve Moore over by the playground on Ocean Boulevard. Steve's ass was resting against the railing that separated the boardwalk from the beach. I was facing him. A breeze off the ocean made the air smell salty.

"Why the hell didn't you call 911 the minute Ferguson and his buddies left?" Steve asked.

I listened to the squeals and laughter coming from the children in the playground for a long moment before answering. I was frustrated, but I did my best to keep it out of my voice. "I told you, she was petrified. It's not only her she's worried about, it's her daughter. And after what I've seen of Ferguson and the other two, I don't blame her."

Two rollerbladers, one a cute blonde, whizzed by. Steve's eyes followed the blonde. "You want to file a complaint?"

I shook my head. "I'm worried too. About what they might try." I quickly added, "Not to me. To Tammy and her daughter."

I could tell Steve knew I was more than a little concerned for my own safety, too.

He shrugged. "Without the woman, it wouldn't do much good anyway. It would be a 'you said, he said' situation. Maybe a little internal investigation. But that would be a laugh. My best advice to you, which I always seem to be giving, is to drop the whole thing. Forget about Ferguson. Think more about making fancy summer drinks."

He gave me a scowl and added, "And staying sober. You look like shit."

I felt heat rise in my face. Whether Steve knew I'd used coke again or not, I didn't know. I hoped the sober remark referred just to booze. "I can't just drop it, Steve. Gant's still got me pegged for the Mariani murder. I gotta clear myself."

Steve pushed forward off the railing, came close to my face. "For Chrissake, Dan, I told you before—let it go. The investigation will point in another direction before long and Gant'll be forced to forget about you. Don't you ever learn?"

Sometimes I wondered that myself. If I ever learned, that is. And the answer was always the same—apparently not. "I have to stick with it, Steve. I have no choice."

I walked around him and leaned my back against the railing so I was facing his back. Steve stared at the concrete boardwalk and shook his head.

He finally turned and looked up. "What are you going to do?"

I was about to answer when a siren blared. A fire engine, judging by the sound of it. I looked across Ocean Boulevard to one of the side streets a bit south of us. A hook-and-ladder pulled out into the heavy summer traffic and inched its way up the boulevard, the ear-splitting siren causing heads everywhere to turn. The fire engine passed us, the noise deafening. By the time the engine passed the Casino, the noise had receded to a bearable level.

Police cars and an ambulance followed within seconds, the racket from their sirens repeating the annoyance. If you were new to Hampton Beach, you'd think the Casino was on fire. As a local, I knew that the sirens rarely signaled anything of importance. They were background noise all day long in the summer.

"I don't know." I had no idea how to proceed. "Just keep poking around, I guess."

Steve harrumphed. "Poking around, poking around. This damn poking around is going to get you killed. You've been lucky it hasn't already. And the more I think about it, I'm not sure how much I can help you. I'm just a town cop. Out of my jurisdiction and all that. If I get involved, and Gant finds out, he'd have me demoted before the next high tide."

He gave me an irritated look. "He doesn't think much of some of my friends as it is."

I felt my face heat for the second time.

Steve's eyes narrowed. I could tell he'd thought of something.

"What?" I asked.

Steve crossed his arms. Took a step closer, so close I could see the pistol bulging under his sport coat. He lowered his voice as much as he could and still be heard over the cacophony of kids' shouts and laughter from the adjacent playground. "I was thinking about this the day after we had our powwow at the White Cap. Do you remember my friend Bill Walkowski from the State Police Major Crimes Unit?"

I nodded. I'd met him once before during an unpleasant incident on the beach.

"Well, he's on some regional task force and knows some Mass state cops. They've been looking into Ferguson for years. But because no one's talking, they haven't been able to prove squat. I'm just wondering if you'd mind me running your tale by him? He might know someone that would be interested."

I thought for a moment but couldn't come up with a reason not to. I was already in over my head. Murder charge plus threats of violence equals time to bring in more help.

"No, not at all," I said.

Steve nodded and looked relieved for some reason I didn't understand. Maybe he was more worried about me than I'd realized and was hoping his state cop friend could protect my ass.

"All right, then. I can't promise anything'll come of it. For all I know, they've closed the books on Ferguson thinking he's too hard a nut to crack. But I'll find out."

"Fair enough," I said.

Out of the blue, Steve asked, "How's Dianne?"

I could tell he was aware of the blowup we'd had by the tone of his voice. How he knew, I had no idea. I couldn't lie to him. He was my friend, and he'd risked his career for me in the past. Besides, I had no reason to lie about this. Not to Steve.

"We're going through a rough patch, I guess."

"You ought to smooth it out," he said. "She's a wonderful woman."

"I know," I said.

Steve cleared his throat, looked around uncomfortably. "You know, Dan, if you ever need help, I'm here for you. I don't know what I could do, but if you need a place to stay for a while . . . or anything."

He knew that too! About the coke. How, I didn't know that, either, but he'd just told me so in the language people use when they don't want to come right out and say it.

Heat rose in my face for the third time. "I know that."

"Kelsey would love to see you. He asks about you all the time."

I smiled. Kelsey, Steve's adopted son. Steve felt I'd saved the boy's life not so long ago. And I knew he would never forget it. I would've enjoyed seeing Kelsey, too, but not like this. The boy looked up to me. I couldn't lose his respect. I'd lost too much already.

"I'll come around sometime, Steve. Tell Kelsey I said hi."

He nodded again. "I'll get in touch with you as soon as I hear anything."

"Okay, thanks," I said.

He turned and started to walk away, stopped, and looked back. "And take care of yourself. Stop thinking everything in the world is your fault. It's not. It's just the way it is."

He turned again and left.

I watched the gaggle of kids in the playground for a while, listening to their giggles and screeches and remembering all the hours I'd spent in there with my own children.

I'd felt like a different person back then. Would I ever feel that way again?

I shook the painful images out of my mind and headed south on Ocean Boulevard toward the Island and my cottage.

Chapter 25

SHAMROCK CALLED AFTER I'd gotten back from the meeting with Steve Moore. He asked if I'd like to meet for a drink. Nine p.m. found us sitting at a small table near the front windows of the Crooked Shillelagh. The place was quiet. That would change in an hour or two; the bar usually became a madhouse on summer nights. But right now, with no music or din from a drunken crowd to disturb us, we could actually hear each other talk.

"You really did it this time, Danny, my boy," Shamrock said.

"That much I know."

"Well, it's not really *that* bad," he said, pulling back, concern stamped on his freckled face. "You know how the lassie can be."

"Dianne's never told me not to come back *period* before."

"Aye, but she's a fiery woman, Danny. And you hurt her. It'll take her a little while to calm down."

I took a sip from my mug of Heineken. It tasted stale, though it probably wasn't. "What has she said to you?"

Shamrock took a swig from a mug of his favorite—dark, thick Guinness—and made a show of sighing and licking his lips. He wasn't fooling me. He was worried about me, that I could tell. And he wanted to make sure he didn't say anything that might push me closer to the edge.

Finally, he said, "She's pissed all right, no getting around that. As any lady like Dianne would be. You disappointed her, Danny."

He must have seen some reaction in my face he didn't like because he shifted gears quickly. "But it's not that big a deal. Look at me. I've taken the pledge more than once after a bad drunk and been stupid enough to tell people about it. After a few days, I feel like a new man. So, off the wagon I go. More than a coupla people been disappointed in me, too, I'm sure. But they always forget about it, sooner or later."

I shook my head slowly. "This is different and you know it. I lost my freakin' family and my kids, Shamrock. Plus the High Tide and my money. Almost my life. Now I may have lost Dianne. I must've been out of my mind to do that stuff again after all this time."

Shamrock looked at me sternly. "Aye, Danny, that's it. You were out of your mind for a day. Temporary mental derangement. But look!" He pointed a scarred white index finger at my chest. "You stopped. You did it. That couldn't have been easy."

Glumly, I said, "It wasn't hard either. It's not like the old days when I'd go berserk for a week. Now I'm so worn out I only go insane for a day. That didn't take any willpower. My body just can't take it anymore."

Shamrock brightened up, but I could tell it was a bit forced. "You see, you just slipped for a day. Nothing more. Could happen to anyone."

"But it happened to me. And I'd promised her . . . I promised myself. And I'd been clean so long. Now, maybe, she's gone."

Shamrock raised his mug and jiggled it, signaling for the barmaid. "Ahh, for the love a Mary, get off your damn pity pot, Danny. It'll blow over. I'll talk to Dianne." He banged a thumb against his chest. "I'll tell her it was just a one-day hiccup. That you're good now, fine as a man can be. Off the stuff for good, too."

I didn't mind him talking to Dianne. She loved Shamrock. And I figured the way she felt about me now, he couldn't make it any worse.

"Danny, you are . . ."

He stopped. I coaxed him into continuing even though I knew what he was going to say.

"You *are* off the devil powder for good, aren't you?"

I felt the corners of my mouth sag. "I couldn't have gotten out of the cottage if I wasn't."

He nodded. "I know that. Jaysus, I know that. But you're going to stay off it, right? You ain't tempted? Cause if you are, I could stay with you, or vice versa. You know. Just 'til you get over the bad part."

I felt like jamming coke up my nose as much as I felt like jamming a railroad spike up my ass and I told my friend so.

Shamrock beamed, though the smile still looked forced.

"Good," he said just as the barmaid came with our fresh beer. She was young and could have easily passed for Shamrock's sister.

"Here yer go, gentleman," she said with a brogue that made Shamrock's speech sound like he was born here. She set down another Guinness for Shamrock and a Heineken for me.

"You're a cute little lassie," Shamrock cooed, making eyes at the pretty redhead.

She smiled a wonderful smile—Irish through and through—and shook her finger at him. "Be good, Shamrock, or I'll have ta shut yer off."

I felt a bit, just a bit, more cheerful. "You'd go bankrupt if you did that."

She turned that wonderful smile on me.

"Aye," she said softly, "and that's no blarney."

We both watched her as she sashayed away.

Shamrock turned to me. "Now that we've got this all squared away—I'll use my magic on Dianne and everything will be beautiful again—what was it you said you had to tell me when I called?"

I told him about my encounter with Ferguson at Tammy's house, the whole terrifying story. I wasn't frightened as I told him about almost being murdered. After all, I had the cocaine blues bad and depression put a damper on fear.

By the time I wrapped up my little speech, Shamrock's eyes were the size of the dinner plates at the Tide.

He took a huge gulp of his beer, almost choked, then sputtered, "Jumpin' Jaysus, Daniel. Can this get any goddamn worse?"

He held up his hand, made it shimmy. "Please don't answer that."

"I don't know," I said, ignoring the request. "I don't particularly care if it does right now. I'm finding out who killed Mariani. To clear *both* our names."

Shamrock looked a bit jittery. "I'm not sure that's so important anymore."

He craned his neck in the direction of the bar. "Where the hell is that cute vixen when you need her?" He looked at me. "Want another?"

"I haven't even finished my first." I glanced down at the full beer and the half-empty mug on the table in front of me. The beer still tasted foul. As foul as my mood.

"Christ, you *must* be a hurtin' puppy. But it'll pass. It always does." Shamrock caught himself. "I mean, it always used to a long time ago."

He rushed to change the subject. "What are you going to do now?"

"I don't know. Something'll come to mind."

Shamrock frowned. "That's what I'm afraid of."

He was right to be afraid.

I'd have to fight to control the dangerous way I was feeling or I'd make a bad situation worse.

Chapter 26

THE NEXT MORNING, I was out on my front porch in my rocker with a coffee. The weather was nice. A few puffy clouds, 85 degrees, no humidity. I hadn't shaken the depression yet, or begun to feel human, but I was feeling a little bit better than yesterday. That was how it would play out—how it always played out. A little better every day.

If I could just hang in there.

I was running a useless loop through my head about what a piece of shit I was when a car pulled up on the street in front of my cottage. Other cars had come and gone in the past hour, all looking for non-existent parking on the dead-end street. I lived close to the beach and was used to the traffic.

This car was different, though. A dark Ford. Even from this distance I could see the foot-high antenna on the trunk.

A cop car.

My heart sped up a bit as the car pulled into a no-parking spot. The door opened and out stepped someone I didn't recognize. He came down the walkway to my house and up the steps to the porch.

"Dan Marlowe?" he said, offering his hand.

"Yes," I said as we shook.

"I'm Sergeant Jack Masterson, Massachusetts State Police." He flashed his identification.

"Have a seat." I motioned for him to take the rocker beside me and he did, adjusting the gun on his hip so it wouldn't dig into his side. He appeared to be in his forties, about my height but a bit heavier. He wore a lightweight sport coat, slacks, and no tie. His gray hair was styled in the standard cop buzz-cut. His face was slightly florid.

"Want something to drink?" I asked. "Coffee? Beer?"

"No, no thanks. I already had my morning jolt. And no beer on duty."

"What can I do for you?" I asked, although I was pretty sure I already knew.

"I heard you might have some information on a certain Salisbury cop."

"Boy, you and Steve are fast."

"Steve?"

"Steve Moore. Hampton police."

"Oh, yeah . . . ahh, sure. Nice guy." He hesitated like he might be gathering his thoughts, then continued. "I've found if you let something cool down, it often burns right out. Something I'm interested in, that is. And *this* I'm very interested in. Why don't you tell me about it?"

So I told him the whole story—the theft of Dianne's jewelry, the Mariani murder, Lieutenant Gant's belief that I was the killer, the visit I'd had from Ponzie and the Ape, Ferguson going in the back door of the pawnshop, the fire at Shamrock's house, and my encounter with Ferguson and his gang at Tammy's house. The only thing I didn't mention was the cocaine.

Masterson didn't interrupt. When I was done, the morning went silent.

"It's a beautiful location you got here," Masterson finally said. "You must enjoy it a lot."

I stifled a snort. "Most of the time." I waited a heartbeat, then added, "What do you think about what I just told you?"

"Ferguson's a scumbag. A crooked cop. But I already knew that. What I'm trying to come up with is a way to use your info to nail the guy."

"How would you do that?"

He turned to me. "You know all this is confidential, and you'll keep quiet about it, right? Even with your cop friend."

"Of course."

"I had to ask, even though Bill Walkowski told me what kind of person you are," he said, referring to the New Hampshire state cop.

That made me feel a notch better. I waited for him to continue.

"You probably already know this, but we've been trying to nail Ferguson for a long time." Masterson scowled. "We've had no luck. And that's unusual. We can most often turn somebody when we want a dirtbag this bad. But over in Salisbury? With him? No luck. The couple of informants we've had through the years desperate enough to give it a try either disappeared or ended up in the marsh."

"Mariani!"

"I didn't say that."

He didn't have to.

"I would love to have your help bringing down Ferguson, Dan."

He kept talking, but I wasn't listening. If Masterson knew Sal Mariani had been killed by Ferguson or his underlings, he also knew Shamrock and I had nothing to do with the crime. When he was done talking, I told him that.

"I didn't mention Mariani's name, Dan. You did. I would never mention the name of someone working with me, not that I'm saying Mariani did."

"But you didn't say he *wasn't* working with you, either."

"No, I didn't."

I leaned forward in my rocker. "But if he was working with you and you had a good idea Ferguson killed him, you could get Lieutenant Gant off our backs. Shamrock and me."

"I can't do that, Dan. I won't jeopardize an ongoing investigation." He stared over my shoulder toward the dunes and the state park. "Of course, if I could get Ferguson in a jackpot somehow . . . well, that might make a difference. I wouldn't really have an investigation to protect anymore, would I?"

His gaze turned toward me, though his question wasn't really a question. He *knew* we hadn't killed Sal Mariani. And he wasn't going to help me clear my name until I helped him corral Ferguson.

I doubted that Masterson would keep the fact of our innocence quiet when push came to shove. But I couldn't risk that I was wrong. He was probably so used to working with lowlifes and rats that this was how he always did it. He couldn't imagine that anyone would be as committed as I already was. Especially with all the danger involved.

But I was. Committed, that is.

"What do you want?"

A satisfied look came on his face. "Just to run some intelligence by you. Make sure I'm on the right track. That I'm not looking at innocent people. Maybe a couple of other small things. Would you do that?"

"I guess."

Masterson's smile turned to a frown. "There's one little speed bump. Like I said, the few people we've been able to get near Ferguson have gone kaput one way or another. It might take me a while to dig up someone else that he, or at least his boys, might trust."

He looked at me as if expecting me to say something.

When I didn't, he continued, "Unless you know someone we could use?"

I told him who I had in mind. He reluctantly gave me the green light.

Chapter 27

"WORKING WITH THE cops? Us?" Eddie Hoar couldn't have looked more scared if I told him he was about to be tossed into a woodchipper.

Shamrock and I were back at Eddie's aunt's house in the mobile home park in Seabrook.

"Yes, you," I answered. "Both of you."

Eddie's aunt was still away on one of her many Florida outings. As usual, Eddie and Derwood had made a mess of the tidy little house. Empty pizza boxes, beer cans, and other debris littered the place—normal when these two commandeered the premises.

I was sitting on the couch with Shamrock. Eddie and Derwood sat across from us on matching chairs.

"When I gave you that money to pay your drug dealer," I said, "you promised you'd help me when I needed it. And you're here, so I must've saved your life. I'm not asking much, considering."

Eddie straightened his shoulders and morphed from scared to indignant. "But me . . . Eddie Hoar . . . helping the cops?" He sounded as if the thought seemed as bizarre as the flat earth theory.

"But Eddie," Derwood said. "What about the time you got caught with them parking meter heads and you worked those charges off and the time you . . ."

"Shut up, Derwood." Eddie blushed a bit. "That was more a civic duty type thing." He looked at me, then at Shamrock. "I just got . . . ahh . . . misguided . . . yeah, that's it. I got misguided one night, had a little too much to drink, and swiped a meter. Ha, ha. Just a little indiscretion. But I helped the cops round up a gang that was stealing meters faster than the town could put 'em up. You can't have people stealing a city's revenue, can you? Now that I think of it, I saved you a lot in taxes."

"But, Eddie," Derwood went on as if unconvinced. "What about the time you . . ."

Eddie swatted his hand at Derwood. "Forget that stuff, will ya? Sometimes I wish I was bigger than you. Why . . . I'd, I'd . . ."

"Knock it off, Eddie," I interrupted. "I'm tired of your bullshit. Especially now. And now that I think of it, your so-called *indiscretions* mean that you have experience working with the police. *And* you owe me."

"Damn right you owe Danny, squealer." Shamrock said.

"All right, all right," Eddie said reluctantly. "I'll help. But I ain't gonna do anything that'll get me hurt."

"We'll be with you all the way," I said. "And you'll have police protection, too."

I had no idea if that last statement was true or not. When talking to someone on Eddie's level, little moral niceties like not lying had to go out the window at times.

"Ahh, okay, I guess," Eddie said.

"All right then—" I began.

"Before you do a big speech, I gotta go to the can," Eddie said.

I sighed. "Okay, hurry up."

Eddie popped up off his chair like his bladder was about ready to burst. All three of us watched him go.

"Hey, Dan," Derwood said. "You won't need me for this, will you?"

"Yes, I will, Derwood. If you remember, when I gave the money to Eddie you promised to help me if I needed it because the dealer would've come after you, too."

"But I ain't got no experience like Eddie, being a ra . . . an informer, I mean," Derwood whined.

"Don't worry about that," I said. "We'll give you on-the-job training."

Derwood frowned. "I won't be any good."

"You'll be fine," Shamrock said, a big grin on his face. "The biggest grasser on the seacoast will be with you."

Derwood looked puzzled. "Grasser? Grasser? You mean a lawn—"

"He means the biggest informer. Eddie," I said.

Derwood frowned. "Oh."

I looked in the direction Eddie had gone. "Where the hell is he anyhow?"

Shamrock jumped up. "Maybe the eejit went out the bathroom window."

"No," Derwood said, shaking his head. "He's having a little taste. Eddie likes to have a little taste before business. Says it makes his mind sharp."

"Sharp?" Shamrock exclaimed. "His mind's as sharp as a butter knife."

He headed for the bathroom. "I'll get the dunce."

Once around the corner and out of sight, I could hear Shamrock banging on what was surely the bathroom door. "Come out of there, you imbecile, or I'll break the door down."

Fortunately, it didn't come to that. In less than a minute, Eddie strolled into the room with Shamrock behind him, glaring at Eddie's back.

"He's wired, Danny," Shamrock said, taking his seat.

"I am *not* wired," Eddie said as he sat down.

All I had to do was study the man for a bit. The longer I stared at him the more he wiggled around like his ass was on fire. His jaw muscles were just as jerky as were his eyes.

I was sure Eddie's drug of choice was meth. Not my preference. The fact he'd just done what he'd done didn't tempt me at all.

I moved ahead. "We're going to have to come up with something between us that'll work. Get us close to Ferguson."

Eddie leaned forward like he might spring from the chair. "I got an idea."

"Great," Shamrock said, rolling his eyes.

"You give me a load of gold jewelry and I go into the pawnshop and then you and the cops come chargin' in and arrest them all. How's that?" Eddie shook his head, looking from one of us to another, a bizarre grimace on his face.

"Forget that, Eddie," I said. "Going into their pawnshop with a load of gold would set off alarm bells. Besides, Ponzie doesn't like you."

"Ponzie doesn't like anybody unless there's money to be made. Then you're his best friend. Right, Derwood?"

"He's right about that," Derwood answered.

"That's no good, Dan," Shamrock said. "Eddie'd pocket half the jewelry before he got in the store."

"That's probably true," I said. "But it's a lame idea anyway. Number one, we wouldn't be getting Ferguson. Number two, possession of stolen goods probably wouldn't be a heavy enough charge to get Ponzie and his wife to flip on Ferguson. We've got to come up with something else."

We sat there for a long while—the three of us still and silent. Eddie was anything but still. He fidgeted, wore out the carpet with trips to the bathroom, and almost drove Shamrock to violence with his crackpot ideas. Then he said it.

"Why don't we just get him with some crank?" Eddie said.

"Ponzie?" I said. "He deals meth?"

"Well…yeah," Eddie said as if he wished he hadn't.

It didn't surprise me. It made sense. Sal Mariani was into meth. Probably Ponzie's and maybe even Ferguson's. That was why they were so concerned about me nosing around. They were moving meth, not just stolen goods. They were worried I'd expose their dope dealing.

"Why didn't you tell me this before?" I said.

"You never asked," Eddie answered.

"Tell him the truth, Eddie," Derwood interjected. "Eddie sometimes gets his stuff from Ponzie or one a his people. He didn't want anything happening to his connection."

Eddie glared at Derwood.

"Does Ferguson have anything to do with it?" I asked.

"I dunno, but I always figured he did," Eddie said. "Him and Ponzie being so tight."

By the end of our visit, we managed to come up with a plan of attack which would—if all went well—bring down Mikey Ferguson and his gang.

Provided we weren't all killed in the attempt.

Chapter 28

I HADN'T BEEN able to come up with a way to get directly to Ferguson. Sure he had his finger in a lot of pies over in Salisbury, and along the Seacoast too, but he rarely got his hands dirty. He was too smart. We'd have to come at him from a different angle.

Ponzie was that angle. The weak link. That's why I'd called Sergeant Masterson the following day. We met at my cottage. Not outside this time. The cottages were too close together to risk anyone overhearing our conversation. We were in the kitchen, seated at the little table, cups of coffee in front of both of us.

"What do you think?" I asked after telling him what I'd come up with over at Eddie's aunt's house.

He blew on his coffee, took a sip. "You think this . . . ?"

"Tammy," I said.

"You think she'll go along with it?"

"I think so. She knows she's in danger. She knows too much about Ferguson, Ponzie, and the rest of them. I think she'd cooperate for that reason . . . and for her daughter. She'd definitely do it for her daughter."

"Well, a reverse sting . . . it might just work," Masterson said.

"Can you get somebody to play the big supplier?" I asked.

"Oh yeah, that's no problem. I might have to pull in someone from out of state. Ferguson's got connections around here. He'd check out his own grandmother, and he knows how to do it."

"From what Eddie told me, Ponzie'll most likely keep Ferguson in the dark so he doesn't have to cut him in." I leaned across the table and lowered my voice as if someone was listening close by. "He'll be skipping his regular source, so he'll probably figure he can get away without Ferguson knowing."

"We'll still be able to flip Ponzie on Ferguson," Masterson said. "But I can't take a chance that he won't run it by Ferguson, so I'll still have to use someone from out of state."

I leaned back in the chair. "Who will you get?"

"There's a state/DEA task force I can call on. They'll send in the right person. Ferguson won't be able to break this guy's beard. He's good, and he'll play Ponzie like a Stradivarius. What I am worried about is this Hoar guy. He sounds about as reliable as a Chevy Chevette."

I grimaced. "Well, I got one—a Chevette, that is—and it's not too bad. Neither is Eddie. He can do it. He's done this kind of thing before. Sure, he's a character, but he lives the life and knows how to talk a clam out of its shell. He can introduce your boy to Ponzie. And Tammy can vouch for the guy."

Masterson let out a big sigh. "It might work. It's worth the effort anyhow, just to get a meth dealer off the street. But Ferguson's the big prize. I want to jack up this Ponzie scumbag big time. You think a pound is too much for him to handle? I don't want to scare him off. We could nail him with a twenty-year mandatory then. That'd make him roll."

I shook my head. "I don't know. Probably not. Let me run it by Tammy. See if she knows how much Sal was buying. We can figure it out that way. I'll ask Eddie, too. He'll know if Ponzie can handle that much."

"Yeah, I don't want to spook him."

Masterson took a pack of smokes from his shirt pocket, tapped one out, and fired up. He took a deep drag and let out a long stream of white smoke, aiming it toward the ceiling. I didn't know a man's lungs could hold that much.

When he was done, he turned his head toward me. "You know, Dan, I'd feel a lot better about this if *you* were the one to introduce my undercover man."

"Me?" I said incredulously. My stomach suddenly felt queasy.

"Yeah, you. Why not? You've got the bona fides."

Sure, he knew about my past. That didn't mean I liked being reminded of it, a past I'd worked years to live down.

Until a few days ago, that is. Still, I didn't want to mix that part of my life with this. Dredge it all up. Keep the old talk going.

Besides, there was something else. "I've never set someone up in my life. I don't like it. I'm not a rat."

Masterson took another hit on his smoke. Quickly this time. "You're not ratting. We already know who they are. Ponzie's a big-time meth dealer and probably a murderer. Ferguson's his boss. Together they've probably ruined hundreds of lives on the beach."

He studied me. When I didn't react, he said, "You could go to jail for a murder they probably committed. It could happen."

That got a rise out of me. But still not enough for me to tell Masterson what he wanted to hear.

"They're going to kill the girl, Dan. Tammy. They can't leave her alive, not with what she knows. If the little one is around when they do it . . ."

"All right. All right." I rubbed my face hard, top to bottom and back again. "Let me think about it."

"You could keep them all in line, Dan. Tammy, Hoar, the bunch of them. Without you around, she could fall apart, and him . . . well . . . who knows? You could save a lot of lives. Even your own."

"I get it." I massaged my temple with the thumb and forefinger of one hand. "I said let me think about it."

"All right," he said, sounding more willing than I would have expected.

That it would come to this hadn't crossed my mind. Even though I'd talked Eddie into doing the same thing, somehow that seemed different. That was Eddie, not me. He did it all the time anyway. Somehow, I'd justified that. I couldn't get around this one though. I had a code and now this cop was asking me to break it. Being a snitch was like doing drugs—if you let yourself be lured in once, you might as well keep on doing it.

At least that's how I'd always looked at it.

But this *was* different. There was more at stake than my reputation and silly code.

Tammy and Amy.

They were in danger. That was one of the reasons I wanted to see Ferguson and Ponzie locked up someplace where they couldn't hurt Tammy or her daughter.

But did I want to get physically involved? In effect, I'd be ratting out not only Ponzie but Ferguson too. And yes, in my book setting someone up was the same as ratting them out. Maybe worse.

I wasn't afraid of physical retribution, believe me. I didn't have much left anyway, not even Dianne. That's why the damn code was so important to me.

But what if Tammy and Eddie couldn't pull it off without me more involved?

Eddie was a loose cannon on his best days. He had the experience needed to set someone up, I didn't doubt that. But someone in Ponzie's league?

And Tammy was a good woman who was a little strung out. Would she be able to keep it together? What if something happened to her? Or, god forbid, to her daughter?

I would be the one to blame, code or no damn code.

Masterson's chair scratched across the floor as he stood up. "You think about it, Dan. Talk to Tammy. I'm going to get things going. Make some calls. We'll have to have a meet with Tammy and Hoar. I'll be in touch."

I didn't even hear him go.

What had seemed like such a good idea just an hour ago, now seemed anything but. Added to the remnants of my cocaine binge, I was just short of chucking it all.

So I went to the living room, picked up the phone and called the High Tide. Dianne answered.

"Hi," I said.

She hung up on me.

My day was complete.

Chapter 29

I DIDN'T DO anything much the next day or two, just putzed around. Kept the beer to a minimum and got back into my morning jogs. Started slow at first, ten minutes. It would take me a while to build up to my usual thirty-minute run. But I'd do it. The cocaine depression was slowly lifting and I felt better every day.

The other thing I accomplished was to set up the meet that Sergeant Masterson had suggested. Which was why I found myself in an old blue barrel chair at Tammy's house come early afternoon two days later. Tammy sat across from me in the only other chair in the living room. On a sofa facing us sat Eddie Hoar and Derwood Doller. They looked like they were waiting for their execution.

We'd decided to have this get-together here so Tammy wouldn't have to get a babysitter for her daughter. Amy was in her bedroom. I could hear her talking to her dolls—or so I assumed.

We were all nervously waiting for the final attendee to show up. A soft rap on the door, announced his arrival.

Tammy got up, let him in.

Sergeant Masterson strode to the middle of the room and nodded at me. I made the introductions all around. Masterson didn't look thrilled when he glanced at Eddie. Not many people did.

"I didn't hear you pull up," I said.

Masterson cocked his head. "I parked around the corner, on Ashworth, in a motel lot. It's an unmarked but not to someone like Ferguson. Didn't want to take a chance."

Eddie, Derwood, and Tammy were all silent. Masterson looked down at us like he was a teacher about to address his students.

"I don't know how much Dan has told you all about this." Masterson looked at me.

I shrugged. "They know about as much as I do."

"Okay, then." Masterson folded his arms across his chest. "We're going to set up this Ponzie dirtbag."

He looked at Tammy. Her eyes were misty.

"He's been involved in more than hot goods on the seacoast," Masterson continued. "Dope and probably even murder."

Tammy sniffled.

"We're going to get Ponzie jammed up good." His tone changed to that of a coach giving a pre-game pep talk.

No one reacted.

Except Eddie who was squirming in his chair like a worm being threaded on a hook.

Masterson took note of Eddie's condition too. Judging by the frown on Masterson's face, he didn't like what he saw.

Masterson took a couple of steps closer. He was just about standing in the middle of our little group. "I don't know if Dan told you this, but Ponzie isn't my main target. It's Sergeant Ferguson."

I'd told them, but Tammy gasped anyway.

"That's why I want Ponzie jacked up on a sizeable meth charge. So he'll roll over on Ferguson. We know Ponzie sells meth. You know that too."

He looked at Tammy. She nodded timidly.

"How much was your boyfriend buying from Ponzie?"

Tammy looked at me. She was scared.

I nodded.

"An ounce or so, I guess," she said, sounding more like a frightened rabbit than the woman who'd saved my life.

"An ounce?" Masterson said, shaking his head in disgust. "That's not gonna be enough to get him to flip on Ferguson. I *want* Ferguson." He said the last three words like it was our fault he didn't have Ferguson, yet.

Eddie looked like he was ready to bolt for the door. Probably was wondering how he'd ever let me talk him into this situation.

No matter what he was thinking, Eddie didn't have time to make a run for it.

Masterson looked in Eddie's direction. "What the hell do you know about this?"

"Me?" Eddie's voice cracked, and he cleared his throat. Derwood sank into the sofa beside Eddie.

"Yeah, you," Masterson said loudly. He quickly turned back to Tammy. "Your husband never bought more than that from Ponzie?"

Tammy shook her head. "I don't so."

Everybody's voice seemed to be cracking. I cleared my throat.

Masterson put his hands on his hips, pushing back his sport coat. You could see the automatic on his hip. Had to wonder if he'd exposed the gun on purpose.

"I hear you know a lot of what goes on with that stuff, Mr. Hoar," Masterson said. "What do you think? Can Ponzie handle more than an ounce or two of meth? A pound maybe?"

Eddie looked at me. I shrugged.

Masterson said, "It wasn't him. I knew about you anyway. So what do you say?"

Eddie jumped to his feet. "I say I'm gettin' outta here. I ain't setting up Ponzie *and* Ferguson for no lousy couple a hundred bucks."

If a man could have looked any more terrified than Eddie did, I'd never seen it.

"Come on," Eddie said to Derwood. "We're going."

Before Derwood could react, Masterson growled at him. "Don't move a muscle."

At that point in time, he didn't look anything like your friendly neighborhood cop. "Sit the fuck down." Masterson took a step toward Eddie and shoved him in the chest.

Eddie was propelled backward and collapsed on the couch beside Derwood, who wasn't moving a muscle.

"Excuse my French," Masterson said to Tammy. She glanced toward her daughter's bedroom without a word. It was quiet in there. Tammy got up, walked over, said a few words into the room, closed the bedroom door, and returned to her seat.

Eddie looked at Masterson with frightened eyes. "You . . . you . . . you can't keep me here. I know my rights."

Masterson chuckled. "Go if you want, Hoar. But before you do . . ."

He reached into an inside pocket of his sport coat, pulled out some papers, and unfolded them. He took glasses from another pocket and perched them on his nose. "You've been a very helpful boy, Eddie."

I had a feeling I knew what was coming.

"Let's see. About three years ago the ATF busted the vice president of the Lawrence chapter of Lucifer's Hammer Motorcycle Club. Got him holding automatic rifles. Couldn't have been done without the help of a confidential informant though. Let's see—his name was . . ."

"All right. All right," Eddie interrupted. He licked his lips, looking from Masterson to each of us in the room. I was afraid he'd snap his skinny neck.

Masterson looked over his glasses at Eddie. "Don't worry, Eddie. You've got nothing to worry about."

When he said that, I knew Eddie had plenty to worry about.

Masterson continued. "Well, as long as these papers never . . . say . . . get lost. Especially got lost in somewhere . . . somewhere like Lawrence. On Aborn Street maybe."

I didn't need anyone to tell me what was most likely on Aborn Street—Lucifer's Hammer's clubhouse. The whimper I heard from Eddie told me I was right. He was in a pickle now. The shaking, shivering, skinny mass of human flesh called Eddie Hoar sitting across from me looked like he'd be too afraid to turn in a jaywalker.

Eddie must have been temporarily insane at the time he'd tossed the biker under the bus. No matter what the cops had on my acquaintance.

Lucifer's Hammer? Someone had to be crazy to squeal on them.

Apparently, Derwood knew nothing about it. "Eddie, you never told . . ."

"Shut up, Dumwood," Eddie said, sounding like his old self for a moment.

Derwood was so shocked—Eddie had ratted out the Hammers—that he didn't make his usual objection to Eddie's use of the insulting name.

Masterson folded the papers, put them back in his pocket. Did the same with his glasses. "Now how about it, Mr. Hoar? Can Ponzie handle a pound of meth without us tripping alarm bells?"

Eddie looked at the floor, nodded a couple of times. He was a broken man. A shell of his former self, which hadn't been much to begin with. But I couldn't blame him. Christ, if the Hammers found out what Eddie had done, he'd be hacked up into little pieces, sealed inside a fifty-five-gallon drum, and dumped in the ocean.

"Can I go?" Derwood asked. "I didn't have nothin' to do with no guns or bikers. That was all Eddie."

Masterson let out a little chuckle. "Nice try, big guy. But everyone knows you're Eddie's partner. If this got out . . . ," he tapped his jacket pocket, "they'd figure you were involved too."

I'd used that same angle on the two hustlers earlier. This cop was good. But not too ethical.

Derwood grabbed his thighs, let out a deep sigh.

That's how the rest of the meeting went, Masterson explaining what everyone was going to do whether they wanted to or not. When Tammy objected out of fear for herself and her daughter, Masterson told her the facts of life. I didn't like the way he said it. That she'd be killed sooner or later anyhow because of what she already knew. And if her child was with Tammy when she got popped, they might do the girl too. It was cruel, but it was true.

By the time the meeting was over, everyone in the room looked like they felt the way I did—that they ought to make out a will. Or flee to Mexico. One of the two. But Mexico was out. And so was the will. There wasn't anyone, except Masterson maybe, who had more than two cents to rub together. Every one of us would have to go all in, play the hand we had and hope we could win this pot.

Unfortunately, none of us had a very good hand.

Chapter 30

THE REVERSE STING began simply enough. Tammy got in touch with Ponzie and told him that Sal had occasionally been buying meth from another dealer, with weight, good prices, and dynamite product. The dealer had smuggling connections. She'd put Ponzie together with this dealer for a small amount of the product for herself.

Ponzie wouldn't be stupid enough to jump right on it—we knew that—but he might very well be greedy enough to get back to her once he mulled the prospect over for a while. Now all we could do was hope Ponzie would take the bait.

Until that happened, we just had to sit tight.

Time enough to visit the High Tide.

I knew Dianne still didn't want to see me, but I didn't care. I had to try and straighten this out. I'd let enough time pass that the negative effects of my cocaine binge had evaporated a good deal. I even smiled at a couple of the passersby who looked familiar as I headed up to the Tide.

It was a nice morning, around 11:00. I strolled up Ocean Boulevard, enjoying the morning for the first time since the binge. The traffic was already bumper-to-bumper, and the shops along the way were doing good business. I nodded to an Indian man busy arranging a series of racks loaded with T-shirts on part of the sidewalk closest to the front of his store. I stopped and chatted with the couple who ran the temporary sunglass stand in front of a motel. They couldn't chat long. They were doing a bang-up business.

When I reached the Tide, I didn't go down the side street to the back door. Not just yet. Instead, I went to the front, studied the building. I don't know what I expected to see. The place hadn't changed in a couple of decades. The front of the building was festooned with lobster traps, buoys, and seagulls along with other maritime knickknacks. There was a small grotto with a fountain near the entrance door, loaded with change, mostly pennies, dropped in by people making a wish.

I smiled as I thought of all the times I'd chased away kids I'd caught dipping their hands in the water and pilfering the change. Sometimes, I guess they got away with it. But that was okay. I imagined they spent the coins up at Funarama. Technically speaking, the money got recirculated in the beach economy.

The front door of the restaurant flew open and Eli came out. He was in his painter's outfit including dirty hat. Paulie followed him, with his long hair and post office shirt as usual. They were a real Mutt and Jeff team. Paulie was about as tall as me while Eli came up to our chests. They both had smokes going. I figured they must have spotted me through the front window. They came up to me, and Eli got right down to business.

"Heard you went on a goddamn toot. Lost your goddamn job. What the hell were ya thinkin'?" Eli said.

Paulie took a fast drag on his butt and blew smoke rings skyward. They floated away on the gentle breeze.

Shamrock and Dianne certainly wouldn't have told them, but I wasn't surprised that Eli and Paulie knew what had happened. My two favorite customers knew my background, they would've put two and two together. Both men were very perceptive.

It didn't bother me much, though. If they knew, then probably half the beach knew. I deserved it. I'd done it to myself. Not Eli. Not Paulie. Not Dianne. Not anyone. Me. And I had to live with the payback.

I didn't answer Eli. What the hell could I say? I put on a stupid grin and shrugged.

"So ya . . ." Eli began before Paulie interrupted him.

"So how you been, Dan?" he said as if I'd just returned from vacation.

"Not bad. How about you guys?"

I should have known enough to keep talking, not to give the floor to Eli.

"We're good," Eli said irritably, "but forget that. We're worried about you. Nobody, not even Dianne or the mick'll tell us what's goin' on with you."

I wanted to interrupt him, but there was barely a breath between his sentences.

"Now look," he continued, holding his cigarette between nicotine-stained fingers beside his face. "The last we heard you and the Irishman were being blamed for Sal the Crapper's murder. And we both been worried about that. Ain't we?"

He turned to Paulie, who nodded, but he didn't stop talking. "Nobody'll tell us nothin' no how. Like we'd blab it all around. We was just worried, that's all."

Paulie took another big drag. Smoke rings floated skyward.

"Now we hear that you fell off the wagon," Eli said, "ya went crazy and lost your job."

I tried to interrupt. "I didn't go crazy, I—"

Eli talked right over me. "And worse we ain't got no good bartender. We're stuck with . . . Bill . . . Bob . . . err . . . whatever the hell his name is."

"Bernie," Paulie threw in.

Eli waved his cigarette. "Yeah, yeah, Bernie Smernie. Whatever. He makes my draft half foam. Half a goddamn glass of foam and when I demand my right to a full glass a beer, he gets all defensive. Ain't that right?"

He looked at Paulie who shrugged.

"And you said yours was warm," Eli said. "But you don't say nothing 'bout it. I say plenty." He tapped his chest with his free hand.

"So when you coming back, Dan?" Eli waved at the building. "The place is going to hell in a handbasket."

I waited a moment, this time making sure he was done with his little speech. "I'm not sure, but I'm hoping to talk to Dianne about it. She here?"

"Yeah, in the kitchen or her office," Paulie said.

Eli jumped back in. "And boy has she been a bit . . ." He caught himself. "Of a grump lately. Maybe you two can cheer each other up and the world'll be all beautiful again."

Eli did make me smile sometimes, and this was one of those times. "I'll do my best."

"You do that," he said. Then he looked like a lightbulb went off in his head. "Hey that half a beer he just gave me is probably gettin' warm. And I don't trust that plumber who's sittin' beside me. If he thinks I'm gone, he might swipe it."

Paulie chuckled, shook his head, his long hair swaying. "Believe me, nobody'd steal your beer, old man."

"Who you callin' an old man? I'd work you under the table any day of the week."

Paulie grinned. "How about next Tuesday morning at eight?"

"Ahh, put a sock in it. You know I don't get up that early. I don't know about you, but I'm going in while I still got a half glass of warm beer." Eli glanced at me. "So long, Dan."

He headed for the restaurant door.

Paulie looked a bit uncomfortable. "Good luck, Dan."

"Thanks," I answered as he followed Eli back inside.

Well, that had been fun. The next conversation I had was sure to be anything but.

I took a last look at the throngs of people traipsing along the sidewalk and the cars inching along the boulevard. Looked up at the beautiful sky—until I got a lungful of exhaust smoke and began coughing—then quickly headed around the side of the Tide and down the street to the back door.

Chapter 31

I FOUND DIANNE sitting in her office, behind her desk. Her hair was pulled back and tied in a pony tail. She had on a white work shirt. I stopped in the open doorway.

"Can I talk to you?" I asked.

She didn't seem too happy to see me. Still, she nodded for me to take the chair in front of the desk.

I closed the door and sat, thankful she wasn't yelling or throwing things at me. That sort of thing had happened in the past. My fault, of course. I wiped suddenly damp palms on my jeans and wondered why I hadn't popped a Xanax before I'd come.

She folded her hands under her chin, elbows on the table, and stared at me. I knew she wasn't going to say anything, so I started.

"I want to know if I can come back to work?"

I'd taken a chance starting with that question. After what had happened since we'd last seen each other, there were probably other subjects on her mind, subjects of more concern to her than me coming back to work. No matter what I said, I was taking a chance. Nothing would have been right. Nothing.

She grabbed the desk with both hands. "You think I'm going to let you come back here and work like nothing happened? You goddamn piece of shit. You promised me you'd never do it again. And here we are again. After everything I did for you."

She'd never referred to me as a piece of shit before, at least not that I could remember anyway. But right about now she was describing how I felt to a T.

I shrank in my chair.

"And that idiot Gant's been here," she continued. "Questioning me and my workers about you. Harassing us."

"Dianne . . ." I started, but she didn't want to hear it.

She went on about everything—things I'd done in the past, things I'd prefer to forget, although of course I'd never been able to. About how I'd promised her and others that I'd never do cocaine again.

About how I'd let them all down.

She could never have me work at the High Tide again. I was untrustworthy. Besides she wouldn't be able to look at what she called my rotten face every day.

She even threatened to call my ex-wife. Tell her I was back on drugs. Someone had to protect my kids from me, she said.

I doubted she'd follow through on that threat. It was just the level her anger was at.

She kept going until I almost couldn't take it anymore.

Finally, she stopped.

I looked up at her. "I guess this means I'm not getting my job back?"

Dianne lunged around her desk like a madwoman. I tried to get up, tipped over the chair, and stumbled back against the wall. She swung her fists, pummeling me in the chest. Dianne was only of average size for a woman, but a few of her punches connected. Though the punches stung, I let her hit me, get it out of her system.

"Dianne," I finally said, keeping my voice soft. "Dianne."

I don't think she heard me. The way she was looking at me, I don't think she saw me either. She was out of control. I tried to wrap my arms around her, pull her toward me, hoping to calm her down before one of her swings did some real damage.

I had one of her arms pressed against her side and was pulling her toward me, when one of her swings caught me in the mouth in a roundhouse punch.

Metal connected with enamel.

I hadn't been hit by a professional boxer, but the blow was hard enough to make my head jerk back.

I grabbed her arm and yanked her close. I guess you'd say I had her in a bear hug. And I wasn't about to let her loose.

She struggled for a long minute, and I had no idea how I was going to get out of this. We'd gone at it before but never like this. I was stupid to come in here in the first place. She'd warned me what would happen if I broke my promise—too many times to count.

I'd gone ahead and done it anyway.

To make matters worse, I'd figured a few apologies and a lot of sweet talk and it'd blow over.

I couldn't have been more wrong.

Someone banged at the door.

"Dianne are you all right?" a man said in accented English. It was Guillermo, the chef.

I could hear Dianne sniffling, feel her panting against my chest. Her body relaxed.

Cautiously, I turned her loose and steeled myself for another blow.

She pulled away from me, looked at me like she didn't know me. "Dan, get out of here and don't come back."

Her face was red and flushed, but there were no tears.

There were drops of blood on her shirt. The coppery taste in my mouth told me the blood was mine.

I walked to the door, opened it. Guillermo stood, hand raised for another knock. His curly black hair glistened with drops of sweat. He stared at me in surprise, his expression quickly changing to one of embarrassment.

I brushed past him and went out the back door, feeling lower than I'd felt in a long time. Lower than even in the past two weeks. Lower than I'd thought a man could ever feel.

Chapter 32

"FOR THE LOVE a Mary! You look like a jack-o'-lantern." Shamrock's face was as shocked as I'd ever seen it.

It was late afternoon the next day and he'd just joined me at Le Bec Rouge, a restaurant on Ocean Boulevard half-way between my cottage and the High Tide. We sat across from each other in a front booth that looked out over Ocean Boulevard. This was an unusual location for us to meet, but I'd picked it because I was uncomfortable at the thought of bumping into people I knew at our usual hangouts.

"Maybe that's better than I looked before," I said, feeling as flat as the joke. I curled my upper lip like a rabid dog so my friend could get a better look at the damage Dianne's ring had done.

"A good size chip. And a front tooth to boot." His brows furrowed. "Who did this to you, Danny? He'll have hell to pay when I catch up with him. Was it Ponzie? One a them? The Ape? Yeah, the Ape. He's big, but we'll give him a good thrashin' for this. Nobody's going to manhandle my best friend. Nobody, why I'd . . ."

I waved my hand in a dismissive gesture, shaking my head. "It wasn't like that, Shamrock."

He looked at me, red brows knitted. "You had an accident?"

I looked down at the table for a moment. I should have just told him, but I wasn't looking forward to it.

A grin spread across his wide face.

"Aye, I know," he said. "You got a bad ice cube. Got into a fight. That's it. Right? I told you before to stay off the hard liquor, Danny. You can't handle it."

I sighed. "That isn't it either, Shamrock. I had an argument with Dianne."

For a minute my friend looked dumbfounded, trying to make sense of what I had just said. Then, he pointed a crooked finger at my mouth. "You mean . . . Dianne did that? To you? Our Dianne?"

"No . . ." I stuttered. "I mean . . . yeah . . . yes, she did it, but she didn't mean to. It was an accident. An accident I deserved."

Shamrock was silent and so was I.

He rubbed the red stubble on his chin. "Danny, I don't know what to say. This is bad. Dianne never broke one of your teeth before. She must've turned all Irish you got her so mad."

I let out a half-assed chuckle and we sat in silence again. Unusual—especially for Shamrock.

Finally, the waitress came and broke the silence. I wasn't hungry and I could tell Shamrock wasn't either. We both ordered a sandwich and Heineken.

"I'll talk to Dianne," Shamrock said when the waitress was gone. "I'll smooth this all out." He hesitated, then added, "She does love you."

"She used to. I don't know about now. It's different this time." I touched my swollen lip. "And not because of this. That's the least of it."

Shamrock let out a very soft, "Aye."

I had to get off the subject before we committed hari-kari together. "I've got news on the Ponzie thing."

I proceeded to bring him up to date on everything new that had happened. He didn't look happy, but at least he didn't look as depressed as he did on the previous subject.

"But what about me?" he said when I was done. "I'm involved in this too. Gant sent someone down to talk to one of my buddies from Ireland. He said the copper was asking him all sorts of questions about me. And trying to see if he thought I'd murdered that junkie."

The waitress appeared with our sandwiches and beers. I poured my Heineken into one of the two mugs she placed on the table. Shamrock took a swig from his bottle.

When the waitress was gone, I continued. "Shamrock, you can take it easy on this one. No sense us all taking a chance when maybe it's not necessary."

"Oh, no," he said, shaking his head. "I'll be damned if that's going to happen. Look at you. You're a mess. You're gonna need me, Michael Kelly, watching your back."

He thumped his chest with a thick beat-up thumb. "I'm your best friend, after all. And look at the scurvy rats you're gonna do this with. Ponzie and the Ape. The Hoar bag and Dumwood. I don't know which pair is worse."

Shamrock was so wound up it would've been useless to try to stop him. "And the cops? Sweet mother of Mary. This Ferguson sounds like he'd steal the bottle from a darling baby if he could sell it somewhere. And who the hell is this state cop? He just wants to make the damn pinch. He doesn't care if your soda bread gets burnt. But I do. I'll have your back. No one'll hurt you if I'm around."

He stopped but before I could speak, he grinned. "Of course, I don't know about Dianne. If she wants to take another poke at you, I . . ."

"Okay, okay. I don't know why I thought I could do this without you. I'll get you in somehow. I don't know how Masterson will take it. We already have a crowded cast—me, Eddie, Derwood, Tammy, and the undercover guy. But I'll talk to him."

"Don't you just talk to him, Danny, you *tell* him. Michael Kelly has more to lose than any of those rascals. Except you. If we go down for this murder, we go down together. Right, Danny? It's always been you and me."

"No one's going anywhere, Shamrock. Especially us. We'll make this thing work and clear our names."

I meant it. As low as I felt, I was determined to get us out of this situation. All in one piece.

Chapter 33

"ME? YOU GOTTA be kidding?" I said. "How the hell am I going to do that?"

I was with Sergeant Masterson, in the front passenger seat of his unmarked car. We were south of the playground, not quite across the street from the Tide, facing the boardwalk and the ocean beyond. A light drizzle meant parking had been no problem.

But there was a problem.

Masterson wanted to use *me* instead of an undercover cop.

I hadn't been overly happy to be involved in his plan to begin with. This made things even worse.

The two-way radio under the dash squawked. Masterson reached over, flicked a switch; it went dead. "It'll be easy. You won't have any trouble. I'll be with you all the way."

I glared at him. He had on shades, and I couldn't see his eyes. I didn't like that for some reason. "What about the professional undercover guy you were going to import from that task force or wherever the hell it was?"

Masterson clucked. "He's tied up. Won't be free for months. We can't wait that long."

"You mean *you* can't wait," I said, still unable to believe what I was hearing. "I can wait."

He let out a heavy sigh. "Afraid you can't, Dan."

"What do you mean by that?" I asked, suddenly wary.

"Ferguson was going to put a hit on the woman."

"Tammy?" I asked, feeling more stupid than usual.

"Yeah, Tammy. But now that she got in touch with Ponzie, she got a reprieve."

I didn't need a weatherman to know which way the wind was blowing. "Ponzie liked what he heard from Tammy. Told Ferguson to keep her alive. Now the two of them would rather get a new meth connection than kill her. For now."

"That's right, sir. You're very good."

I imagined I could see behind his shades and that imagination told me there was a little slyness in those eyes. "Well at least we know he told Ferguson."

"If this deal doesn't happen and we don't get Ferguson and his goons, well, Tammy will be . . . ahh . . . you get the picture."

Yeah, I got the picture. And I didn't like it one bit.

Then Masterson threw another pitch just in case the last one hadn't beaned me in the head.

"And her daughter . . . the kid . . . what's her name? They'll probably kill her too."

I shook my head. "But they're not going to believe I'm a meth dealer. They won't buy that for a minute. They know all about me."

Masterson grinned. "Yeah, they do."

My past was back to haunt me. Again.

I guess it wasn't much of a stretch to think that I might have good crank connections, considering my cocaine history. Sure, they probable knew my past—most everyone on the seacoast did.

But still, crank? Meth?

"They won't believe that," I said.

"Sure, they will," Masterson shot back. "Coke or meth, it's all powder to most people and all green to Ferguson."

I was worried about Tammy and her daughter, but I still doubted that Ferguson would buy that I was, and had been, a big meth dealer. "And I just popped out of nowhere?" I asked.

"I got that already worked out." Masterson wore a smirk on his face.

He thought very highly of himself. At that time, I liked him about as much as I liked Ponzie and Ferguson.

"The past few years you've been going up north," Masterson continued. "Canada. Getting the product from bikers up there. Coming back and selling only to a couple of customers who could take a pound or kilo. Very low key."

I saw a chance to extricate myself from this craziness and seized it. "So how would Tammy know about me? And Sal? He was small potatoes and a junkie to boot. If I was this big-time smuggler, I wouldn't have had anything to do with him."

"Not Sal. But how about his *girlfriend*?" Masterson's smirk turned into a grin.

"You mean . . ."

"Yeah, that's exactly what I mean. You were banging Sal's chick, Tammy. You supplied Sal occasionally as a favor to her."

I shook my head. "They won't buy that."

"Of course they will," he said as if I were a small child. "She's a good-looking chick. Ferguson knows that too. He'll fall for that part easy. He's a freak himself."

I had no idea what he meant by that last reference, and I didn't care. Not at this point. I decided to take a stand. "It won't work. There's no way Ferguson is going to fall for me being a big meth dealer."

Masterson looked like there was something he was about to tell me that he'd prefer not to. He glanced out the front windshield toward the dark water and the just-as-dark sky above it. Without looking at me he said, "You'd be surprised."

I absorbed that for a moment before it finally got through my thick skull. "You've already told him, haven't you?"

He looked at me, cleared his throat. "Tammy has." He paused a moment. "I had to do it, Dan. We couldn't wait months for the undercover to free up. Tammy and her little girl were in danger."

I was steaming but that statement took the head off. "You told her to tell them I was Sal's other supplier? The big smuggler?"

He nodded.

I threw my hands up. "That doesn't mean they'll buy that bullshit."

"They already have," he said softly.

Again, it took a minute for my mind to process the info. "How do you know? From one of your phone taps?"

"That's not important. What's important is that they're buying Tammy's story." He studied me. "You'll save Tammy and her daughter from being killed. Not to mention you might even get off the hook for Mariani's murder. Your buddy, too."

I snorted. "But will it work? I doubt it."

"It's going to work fine." Masterson slapped the top of the dashboard to the rhythm of his words. "I've done this hundreds of times before. Besides, you'll have me and my men watching you at all times. Nothing's going to happen to anybody."

I wished I could have believed that, I really did. Whether I did or not, I couldn't sit by and watch Ferguson turn Ponzie and the Ape loose on Tammy and her daughter, though.

"So that's why you wanted to meet here," I said. "You didn't want to come by my place because Ferguson might be having me watched now."

"Give the man a cigar."

I definitely didn't like this cop. Not anymore. He was too devious. But his was the only game in town.

"I'm going to give you a rundown on how we're going to play this thing," he said. "It'll be beautiful. You ready?"

He didn't wait for my answer, just explained how he was going to run the sting, what everyone's part was going to be, and how they would play it.

"If you expect me to pose as a big-time meth dealer, you're going to have to find a part for one more person," I said when he was done.

He furrowed his eyebrows. "Who?"

"Shamrock. I told you about him."

At first I thought Masterson was going to say no. After a long moment, he smiled and nodded. "Sure. Sure. If that'll keep you happy, I'll find some way he can contribute."

It wasn't going to keep me happy, that I knew. I had an ache in my stomach that told me I might have just signed my friend's death warrant. If I hadn't already promised Shamrock that I'd get him in on the action, I would've left him completely out of it.

Hopefully, this cop knew his stuff and Shamrock and everyone else involved in this dangerous undertaking would get through it alive and in one piece.

Chapter 34

THE NEXT MORNING I got a call from Ponzie. He wanted a meet. Noon time at the pawnshop. I acted reluctant at first. Afraid of violence. I let him assure me there would be nothing for me to worry about. After we finished the charade, I agreed to show up.

I was there on the dot.

Selma was behind the counter just as she had been the first time I'd visited. I walked between the display cases right up to the counter. She looked at me like I was a poor slob hocking his wife's jewelry to pay off his bookie, then nodded her head at a door behind her desk marked *Office*.

I didn't bother to knock, just walked in.

The *office* was a mess, filled with cardboard boxes loaded with what looked like junk. I noticed some used VCRs, old *Life* magazines, lamps and all sorts of gadgets, things I supposed the shop had gotten stuck with through the years and couldn't unload. A couch was against one wall. Ponzie sat across from the couch, behind a cheap, battle-scarred wooden desk. He looked up as I entered.

I pulled one of two gray folding chairs closer to the desk and plunked my ass in it. I hadn't noticed myself being nervous before I'd entered the office. I did now. My heart galloped like an out-of-control race horse and my hands were clammy. I congratulated myself on having the foresight to pop a Xanax an hour earlier; otherwise, the nervousness might have been worse and given my true intentions away.

Ponzie leaned back in his chair, arms across his chest. I noticed a bulge under his shirt near the shoulder. Bandages from the bullet he'd taken at Tammy's, or so I assumed. While he studied me, I studied the tattoo exposed on his forearm. It was either very old or very cheap. The colors were dulled, and I couldn't make heads or tails out of the design. Looking at it kept my mind occupied and my anxiety under control, though.

Finally, Ponzie leaned forward in his chair, put his hairy forearms on the desk and spoke. "Okay, Marlowe. Stand up."

"What?"

He stood and came around the desk.

"Up" he said loudly. "Whaddaya think, I'm stupid?"

I must have been. Stupid, that is. I should have assumed he'd frisk me for a wire.

I stood and Ponzie roughly patted me down. Didn't miss a spot. Even massaged my ass and balls. I didn't like that much. When he was done, he waved at me to sit while he went back around the desk and plopped back into his chair.

"Okay, Marlowe," he began. "I heard you can get some nice product. Tell me about it."

I knew enough about meth from my old days to fake it. Sergeant Masterson hadn't even needed to coach me on that. I let myself go with the flow. "You already know it's good, Ponzie, or you wouldn't have called me."

"How the hell would I know it's good? Because the chick said so?" He snorted. "Or the two jerkoffs, Hoar and his buddy?"

So, he'd reached out to Eddie to confirm Tammy's story. That was good—depending, of course, on what Eddie had said. But if Eddie had blown it, Ponzie would never have called.

I said what a real dealer would've said. "It's the best, Ponzie. Pure."

"Where's it from?" he said quickly.

I grinned. "From me."

Ponzie snickered. "Up north, huh?"

He'd heard about the Canadian bikers. Probably from Tammy or Eddie, maybe both. And that was fine. It even sounded believable to me.

When I didn't answer, he shrugged. "How much?"

"How much can you handle?"

He snorted again. "More than you can probably supply."

"I wouldn't be too sure of that, Ponz."

He gave me a hard look at the nickname. For a long moment, I thought I might have gotten a little too smart.

Finally, he let out a big laugh. "We'll see, Danny."

I smiled back at him. We were buddies now, at least it felt that way. I had to hope he felt the same way.

"How about four pounds, kid? Can you handle that?" He put his hands behind his head, leaned back in the chair again. Smiled.

I was a little surprised at the amount but not unhappy. The more product involved, the more time these jerks would do.

"No problem," I said. I would have said the same thing if he'd asked for four tons. But hopefully he didn't know that.

He leaned in closer, all business now. "All right, how much?"

I had discussed this with Masterson. With any luck the figures we'd come up with were good. We wanted Ponzie to drool, but not be suspicious about the prices. That would spook him for sure.

"Twenty grand a pound." I felt a little quiver in my voice as I spoke. I hoped Ponzie didn't pick up on it. Or, if he did, he'd peg it as normal nervousness. This would be a big drug deal, after all.

Ponzie harrumphed. "You're kidding. That's ridiculous. We're already getting it a lot cheaper."

I didn't miss his use of "we." I hoped he was referring to Ferguson. Time would tell.

"Not stuff like this," I said. "This is the real deal. It's ninety percent *pure*. Made by a professional chemist and not with a bunch of cold tablets either. You can whack it in half, or more, easy."

"So you say."

I reached into my pants, retrieved a one-gram vial with a black cap, and placed it on the desk in front of Ponzie. The vial was half full of a white powder colored by just a hint of gray.

Ponzie stared at it for a minute, looked up at me, and shrugged. He took the cap off the vial, tapped out a mound of the powder. He dug out his wallet, dropped his driver's license and a ten-dollar bill on the table. Then he used the license to form a thick, long line of the powder.

I knew it was almost pure. Masterson had told me so. He also said it had come from the state police evidence room.

If anyone besides Ponzie had cut that big a line, I would have warned them to be a bit more cautious. But if I warned this guy, and he made the dose too small, he wouldn't be convinced how good it was.

So I didn't say anything. It was his funeral after all.

After he'd done a little chopping with the license, he rolled up the bill, placed it inside his right nostril, and hoovered up half the huge line. His head shot up, his eyes popped wide, and he shook his head rapidly.

To my surprise, he shifted the bill to his other nostril and repeated the process with the other half of the line.

He threw his head back and shook it again. His eyes didn't get any wider. If they had, the eyelids would've ripped.

"Not bad," he said. "Not bad. Want some?"

He held the bill out to me.

"No, I haven't slept in a couple of days," I lied. "I got to get some sleep."

He shrugged, dropped the bill on the desk.

I studied him like a scientist in a research lab studies a subject just given an experimental psychedelic drug. His jaw was going a mile a minute, and I could tell he was trying to keep his shit together. Probably afraid if I knew how much it had hit him, I'd jack up the price.

I made some inane comments which he failed to respond to. Finally, he jumped up from his seat.

"How soon can you get this if we want any?"

"Just give me a few days. And that's all cash. No fronts."

He nodded so hard I thought he might hurt his neck. "Yeah, yeah, yeah, yeah, yeah."

He bounded around the desk, glanced at the vial still on the table. "Can I have that? I'll pay ya."

I stood up from my seat. "Keep it, no charge."

I'd planned to leave it anyway. Just in case he wanted Ferguson to try it, even though both Masterson and I figured Ferguson was too smart for that and would rely on Ponzie's seal of approval.

Ponzie grabbed me by the arm and turned me toward the door.

"Yeah, yeah, thanks," he said. His jaw muscles were working so fast I wondered if the man would suffer the first muscle-bound jaw known to man. "We'll call if we like it."

That *we* again.

And as far as liking it—I was pretty sure that Ponzie wouldn't be doing much sleeping for the next few days.

I said goodbye, let myself out, and closed the door behind me.

Selma gave me a bored look as I passed. I felt sorry for her. She didn't know it, but she wouldn't be bored for long. As soon as I was out of the lot, Ponzie would have the joint closed up and Selma in the office with her clothes off and her ass on the couch.

I got a visual. I didn't like it.

On the other hand, knowing the strength of what the pawnshop owner had just shoveled up his nose and knowing the usual outcome, I figured Ponzie's sexual attack on his wife would be nothing more than a very long, drawn-out exercise in frustration.

Hopefully our undercover sting would not turn out the same way.

Chapter 35

AFTER I LEFT the pawnshop, I had lunch and ran a few errands. Then it was time to head for another appointment. This one in Portsmouth. I took Ocean Boulevard—aka Route 1A—up the coast, running into some traffic when I hit M Street. It was a sunny, warm weekday but the traffic didn't delay me too long. Once I got past the Casino, it was easy sailing.

I always enjoyed this drive. It was about as picturesque as you could get in New Hampshire with its short twelve-mile coast.

I slowed down when I reached North Hampton, hitting a speed I maintained through Rye, the next town. As I drove along, I looked from side to side, enjoying the view. On the left were mansions. No other way I can think to describe them. Luxurious homes of all shapes and sizes, all with un-obstructed views of the Atlantic Ocean.

My ex-wife and I had loved to drive this road, scoping out the properties back when we were together and happy. We always wondered what the people inside these castles did for a living. Except for Governor Fuller, we never really knew.

Even now, years later, I had no clue how these people made all their dough. Did more than one of the residents have something illegal in their background? Most people would never consider crossing the line. But you know the old saying—behind every great fortune is a crime. I had to wonder.

Off to the right, waves broke on the expanse of rocks below the road. Beyond that, the Atlantic Ocean. The Isles of Shoals, about twelve miles out, were visible today. I could even make out structures on the islands. Seagulls floating in the air and scattered sailboats completed the nautical picture. It was almost enough to help me forget the predicament I was in. But not quite.

Before I knew it, I reached my destination—downtown Portsmouth. As luck would have it, I found a parking spot only doors from where I was heading. Portsmouth is a beautiful old town on the coast of New Hampshire with a population of about 20,000. Very quaint and somewhat yuppified with art galleries, coffee shops, and eating establishments. A seaport, it was a hub of fishing and, or so I'd heard, smuggling at one time. Maine is only a short hop over a suspended bridge. Portsmouth has more than its share of cozy and interesting drinking establishments. Unfortunately, I had no time for that. Not today.

After parking the car, I fed the meter and walked a short distance to an old colonial-style three-story building. The building hadn't been kept up like most of the properties in the area. Much of the brick facade was faded, cracked, and crumbling in places. I stepped inside and found myself in a small vestibule with a short list of tenants' names below buttons. I didn't peruse the names or press any buttons.

I'd been here before, knew who I was seeing, knew how to get there.

I opened the unlocked inner door and headed up the staircase. The black paint on the railing was chipped, and the railing looked rickety. I didn't need it for assistance anyhow.

When I reached the third floor, I took a right and approached the first door on the left. There was some faded writing on the smoked glass. I didn't need to make it out.

I knocked and a familiar voice said, "Come on in."

I slipped through the door, closing it behind me. The small office I was in was barely bigger than Dianne's at the High Tide. This office was even messier than Ponzie's with boxes of papers scattered around the floor along with a half-dozen filing cabinets, more than one with drawers hanging open. A freestanding coatrack, the kind you don't see anymore unless you watch old private detective movies, stood just inside the door. In a far corner was a refrigerator, one of those little floor jobs kids take to their college dorms and fill with beer. I knew this frig was also filled with beer.

On the wall hung a framed picture of President Clinton. I didn't like that president any more than the presidents that came before him.

The only thing in the room that looked like it hadn't been bought at a garage sale was the big mahogany desk in front of me. It was one of those pieces of furniture you knew had to be expensive, even to a know-nothing like me. In weight alone, the wood must have been worth a lot. Someone could stay warm for a whole winter chopping that desk up and throwing the pieces in a fireplace if their business ever went south.

I'd often wondered if that would ever happen to the man seated behind the desk.

"Sit down, Dan, sit down," my attorney, James Connelly, Esquire said. He was flipping through papers on his desk, apparently desperate to find something. There could be a dead body buried under all that clutter. How could he find anything?

I sat in one of two barrel chairs that faced my lawyer. The chairs weren't as nice as the desk but not as bad as the rest of the office decor.

"What are you looking for?" I asked.

"Someone gave me a check for a bondsman." He threw up his hands in resignation. "It isn't that important right now. I'll find it later."

I wondered if such a check wasn't important to the poor slob sitting in jail waiting to be bailed out with the money his mother or girlfriend had come up with. Didn't surprise me though or alarm me. James was a bit eccentric, to put it mildly.

But he had always come through for me. He'd pulled my bacon out of the fire more than once.

Besides, he worked cheap.

Still, I catalogued his lack of concern for someone stuck in the hoosegow in my mental filing cabinet, under his name, along with a couple of other dicey images I had there.

He sat back in his chair, steepled his fingers under his chin. His curly black hair was just short of the out-of-date Afro style. He had on a wrinkled white shirt, no tie, and a sport coat I had seen a dozen times.

"How the hell do you get yourself involved in these things?" he finally asked.

"It isn't easy." Half joke, half reality.

"No, I imagine it isn't. Beer?" He nodded at the small fridge on the floor.

I shook my head.

James sat straight up, grabbed a pencil off his messy desk, and started spinning it in his fingers. "On the phone, you told me this statie has you playing undercover cop. With meth you said. How much?"

"Four pounds," I answered, my voice shaking a bit.

"Four pounds!" James repeated. "That's enough to put you away in Concord for the duration of your natural life."

"I told you, I'm not the one going to prison. The guys buying it are . . . hopefully."

"What? That's bullshit," James sputtered. "You're holding the dope. That's all it takes for a trafficking charge or possession with intent to sell."

"Yeah, but I'm working with the cop. He said—"

"He said? He said?" James looked at me like I was a dumb sap—which maybe I was. "You know better than that. At least you should. You've been around. The staties want these guys, so they'll just use you. You can't trust any of them. You're just collateral damage if anything happens to you."

James studied me, then his face brightened. "You get anything in writing?"

"Writing?" I felt as if he wanted to know if I'd asked to borrow the cop's service weapon for a few days.

"Yes, *writing*," he said.

I shook my head. "He's not going to give me anything in writing. I told you what he's going to give me. He's going to get me and Shamrock off the hook for the Sal Mariani murder and save an innocent woman and her little girl from being killed. Isn't that enough?"

"*I* can do that," he said confidently. Then he added—less confidently, "I don't know about the woman and her kid, though. That's out of my field. But I'm working on your problem. Give me some time."

"I would," I said, "except the woman doesn't have any time. I've got to play narc soon, or she and her child might die."

James furrowed his brow. "By the way, doesn't that—the playing narc thing—doesn't that violate the *code* you told me about once? You know . . ."

I waved him off. "Yeah, yeah, I know. But what choice do I have? If I don't do this, two people might die *and* Shamrock and I will be charged with murder."

"I just told you . . ."

I waved him silent again. "All right. All right. The woman and her little girl. How can I just let them be murdered?"

James looked exasperated. "How the hell do I know? It's your damn code, not mine. I always thought it was asinine anyway."

"I've lived by it." I could feel my face flush.

"Screw your code." He looked troubled for a moment. "Ironic though."

"What do you mean?"

"I remember you saying an informer always has an excuse for informing."

"They do," I said, finally confident about something. "A rat'll always have an excuse—he ripped me off, he made a play for my wife, he's a rat himself, he belongs to another drug gang. It's always something."

"And now it's the woman and her little girl for you."

"But there isn't any other way to—"

"Look, I'm not your priest or psychiatrist. I'm your lawyer. I take care of your problems out here in the real world.

You got to work out your spiritual and head problems on your own."

He was right, of course. Time to get back on track and talk about what I'd come here to discuss.

So I did and we discussed it. And when I left, I wasn't sure what I'd gotten out of my ride to Portsmouth. Basically, my attorney had said for me to be careful and that he'd look into what we discussed and get back to me.

If you have ever had the unfortunate pleasure of waiting endlessly for a lawyer to get back to you, you probably know how I felt right about then. I could see the future as far as that goes. I'd been there before. I wasn't going to hold my breath for his call. I had to move ahead.

On the ride back to Hampton Beach, the mansions on my right and the ocean on my left didn't brighten my mood as they usually did. Matter of fact, I didn't really see them. I was lost in thoughts about pounds of meth, a little girl and her mother being killed, personal codes being broken, and cramped prison cells. It was enough to make someone veer off the road, down the rocks, and into the ocean. I didn't, though. Instead, I held the steering wheel tight and hoped it would all work out okay. After all, there was only one alternative and I'd just rejected that by keeping the car on the road.

Chapter 36

IT DIDN'T TAKE long to hear from Ponzie. He called the next morning, said we were on. He wanted the four pounds, and the price was agreeable. He sounded like a hamster on a wheel, he was talking so fast. I was sure he hadn't slept yet. That made me smile.

He wanted the deal to go down at Tammy's house. I wasn't sure if Sergeant Masterson would okay that, so I ignored the request. He also wanted people there in addition to me, asking that Tammy, Shamrock, Eddie, and Derwood be there. The same group that Masterson and I had already assembled.

That should have set alarm bells ringing in my head. Dealers generally don't want a peanut gallery around when a deal goes down. But Ponzie claimed he'd feel more comfortable with these folks in the room.

After Ponzie hung up I immediately called Masterson. He must have been waiting by the phone. He told me to meet him that afternoon at Joe's Meat Shoppe in North Hampton for a late lunch. I was familiar with the place; they had a reputation for quality meats.

I hopped in my car about a half-hour before the designated time, backed out of my driveway, and cut through the Island to reach Ocean Boulevard. Just before I turned onto the boulevard, a car pulled out of a side street and fell in behind me. I glanced at it a couple of times, but the car looked innocuous and faded into traffic as we moved along.

Probably just being paranoid, I told myself.

It was another fine beach day, and traffic was medium heavy. I poked along, taking in the sights, biding my time until I reached the Casino. Glancing in the rear view, I noticed the car that had pulled in behind me was still there. I still didn't think much of it. There was only one person in the car. I couldn't make out a face; the visor was down.

When I finally reached the Casino and traffic began to move more briskly, I continued on past the Ashworth Hotel. The car was still behind me, with one or two vehicles separating us.

I decided to do a little counter-surveillance, just to be safe. I banged a right and proceeded up a one-way road that ran around the outside of Boar's Head, a peninsula that jutted about a hundred yards into the Atlantic. There were nice ocean front homes running the entire length of the perimeter of the peninsula and ones almost as nice, but with no ocean view, on the inside of the road. I made a mad drive up the winding street, getting a shout to slow down from more than one resident. Less than a half a minute later, I was back where I started and took a sharp left to make the circle of the peninsula again.

Sure enough, there in front of me, was my tail. I came up until I was only feet behind him. He slowed when he must have seen me in the rearview. We continued our jaunt around the edge of Boar's Head. I wondered how he'd play it when we reached the main drag.

When we reached Ocean Boulevard, my friend observed the stop sign and let a stream of cars pass. It gave me a moment to study the vehicle. It was a non-descript Oldsmobile, dark in color with no identifying marks, antennas, or attachments. I did make note of the New Hampshire license plate, but the figures were obscured by mud.

When the car pulled out onto the road, I fell in behind him. After a short distance, his left blinker went on and he took a turn onto Winnacunnet Road. That would take him to Hampton Center. *If* he stayed on it. I continued north on 1A for a half mile to the next set of lights. I pulled into a small parking lot and planted myself to make sure the car hadn't made a sharp U-turn and started tailing me again. I waited five minutes, and when I was sure he wasn't still following me, I resumed my drive.

Who had been behind me?

I couldn't be sure. Masterson had said he was concerned that Ferguson or Ponzie might have surveillance on me, to see if I was meeting with law enforcement. Or maybe they wanted to see who I got the dope from and cut me out of the deal.

Or maybe it wasn't them at all. Maybe it was the state cops. They might want to make sure I was playing square with them.

I'd have to remember to ask Masterson.

One other thing occurred to me. The wrong person might have heard about the four pounds of meth and $80,000 being in the same place at the same time. There were gangs from Charlestown, Massachusetts, who thought nothing of going into banks with automatic weapons to score a few thousand dollars. The numbers involved in our deal would be very tempting to a lot of bad people.

I finally pushed all the thoughts from my mind. I was getting paranoid. Wouldn't do me any good to worry about it. I just needed to be as careful as I could be and trust no one.

When I pulled into Joe's Meat Shoppe, I saw Masterson's car. I went up the stairs of the old building and walked in. Once in Joe's, I walked by some produce displays and headed for the sandwich counter. Masterson was on my right, seated at one of a half dozen small tables, already eating a sandwich. He nodded when he saw me.

I went up to the counter and ordered a veggie sub. While the young lady made it, I grabbed a diet coke. When she was finished, I paid, walked over to Masterson's table, and took the seat facing him.

"Someone followed me," I said.

Masterson took the sandwich from his mouth, his eyes wide in surprise. He glanced out the window at the parking lot.

"They here?" he asked without swallowing the food in his mouth.

I looked away, disgusted by the sight of half-chewed food. "No, of course not. They knew I'd seen them and headed off toward downtown Hampton."

"You're sure?" he said, chewing the mess in his mouth and swallowing.

"Yes, I'm sure."

"You got a lot of weird friends I've heard. Probably one of them. Nothing to do with this."

I ignored the unintentional insult. I unwrapped my sub and popped open my diet coke. I ate while we talked, making sure to swallow before I opened my mouth.

"Are you sure Ponzie bought the whole story?" he asked.

"As much as I can be. He was still high when he called today." I thought of something else. "Aren't you worried we might bump into Ferguson or Ponzie here?"

"Not likely. I doubt they travel this far north. They like to stay in their little comfort zone. Besides this is quality meat." He held up the end of his sandwich. It looked like rare roast beef. "Good meat to them is from the deli at Market Basket."

My stomach rolled a little at the thought.

"What are we going to do now?" I asked, not sure I really wanted to know.

Even though the tables within earshot were empty, Masterson glanced around. When he was sure there were no invisible people listening in, he continued. "You're going to set it up for three days from now."

"Three days?" I said, my voice cracking. I don't know what I expected, but that was awfully soon. Although if he'd said three months, I probably would have felt the same way.

"Yes, that's all we need to get everything ready for Tammy's."

"Tammy's? How'd you know Ponzie wanted the deal there?"

He hesitated. "That's where *I* want it. Didn't know he'd care where the deal goes down."

"He wants Eddie and Derwood there too," I said. "*And* Shamrock."

Masterson shrugged. "That's no problem. I can make sure the two pea-brains are there. And you wanted your friend to play a role anyway. He can be your partner, a minor partner. It all works out great."

I was uneasy. "Yeah, but this is a lot of people. Why would Ponzie—more importantly, why would Ferguson—want a crowd around? It doesn't seem right."

Masterson smirked. "Look," he said. "Ponzie isn't the brightest bulb on the tree and he's snorting crank."

"Yeah, but Ferguson's no fool, and I doubt he indulges."

He shook his head. "Don't worry about it. I see this type of thing all the time. They just want everybody involved to be there when it goes down. Some of these scumbags work on the theory if everyone is there, nothing'll happen. You know, a rat wouldn't want to be there when the shit hits the fan."

"Maybe," I said, even though I wasn't convinced. Still, Masterson was the expert and he was the only lifeline in sight. I'd have to trust him. I had no choice. "Tammy'll let us do it at her house?"

He nodded. "She will. I'll make sure."

We spent the next forty-five minutes going over the plan. Fortunately, Masterson had finished his food and his mouth was empty of all but teeth and tongue as he talked.

The idea wasn't too involved or original. When we'd talked it all out, we retreated to our cars, and Masterson headed out to wherever cops go when they leave a meeting with an informer.

Informer.

I didn't like that word.

My mind was a jumble on the way back to Hampton, and I felt physically ill. Was it just natural nerves or the start of an anxiety attack?

I didn't know.

I did know I had to forget it for the moment. If it was the beginning of an attack, I'd cut it off before the attack became full-blown. When I reached a place named Runnymeade Farm along the road that led from Joe's back to Route 1 and Hampton, I pulled over to the shoulder of the road, parked, and got out.

I walked up to a shoulder-high, three-rail fence that surrounded a large multi-acre pasture. Directly in front of me was a billboard that announced the farm to be the home of Dancer's Image, a Kentucky Derby winner, later disqualification notwithstanding. I leaned against the fence, watched the famous horse graze and prance around his domain. I didn't know much about horses but this was a beautiful animal. And not a care in the world. He'd won many races, and his work was over. He was retired now, with a better pension than most people received.

By the time I said goodbye to Dancer's Image, my problems had faded into the background and my anxiety was no more. I silently thanked the thoroughbred. How long this positive outlook would last, I didn't know.

Chapter 37

ON THE BIG DAY I was at my cottage. It was late morning. Shamrock was with me. Sergeant Masterson had run through some final instructions, then left to oversee surveillance at Tammy's house. Near the door stood an oversize briefcase, brown in color. Inside were four pounds of methamphetamine. The presence of the drug so close at hand had increased my anxiety level, already high because of the sting we were about to undertake. Fortunately, the Xanax in my system kept my symptoms manageable. Still, my palms were sweating, and I had an unreal sense of dread.

Normal, or the beginnings of an anxiety attack?

In this situation, I couldn't say.

"We should leave, Danny. Time to get going." Shamrock got up from the couch, looked from me to the briefcase on the floor. No restaurant whites today. Instead, he had on jeans and a white sweatshirt with a large green shamrock embroidered on the front. I hoped it would bring us luck.

"Okay." I was already standing. I hadn't sat since Masterson left. I glanced at the case.

"He said you're supposed to hold it, not me," Shamrock said, a very slight quiver in his voice.

Masterson had been adamant about the briefcase and its contents not leaving my sight. Shamrock and I had tossed that back and forth, imagining Masterson had visions of Shamrock absconding with the loot he could get from selling the meth, then heading back to the Emerald Isle or some such nonsense.

I reached over and lifted the case off the floor. Four pounds?

It felt heavier, like it weighed closer to fifty.

Or was it just me again? An anxiety attack bubbling just below the surface?

I clutched the case tight in a hand damp with sweat.

Not much was said between us on the walk up the street.

"I wish I had a gun." Shamrock looked as nervous as I felt.

"I thought you didn't like guns. You like to use your fists when there's trouble."

"Aye, Danny, that's true." Then he added, the slight quiver back in his voice, "But I got a feeling they won't help me much today."

I didn't respond to that; I was nervous enough.

We reached Tammy's house without any more talk. I was so nervous, I guess, that when we walked up the stairs to the porch, I opened the door without knocking. I wanted to get inside somewhere—anywhere—so I wasn't out in the open, four pounds of drugs in my possession.

You would have thought we were Dracula and the Wolfman when we opened the door and walked in. Tammy sat on the sofa, staring at us with eyes the size of full moons.

Derwood lunged half out of his easy chair before he realized it was just us and plopped back down. Eddie, who'd already been on his feet, bolted through the door to the kitchen.

"Eddie, it's just us. Dan and Shamrock," I shouted, knowing otherwise he wouldn't stop until he reached the Casino parking lot.

We all waited. After a minute, Eddie walked back into the living room, a sheepish look on his face. "I thought it might be a rip-off. I was gonna go out the back door and come around front and get a drop on 'em if it was."

"Hah," Derwood said. "You ain't got no piece, Eddie. You're scared of guns. Remember that time you were gonna look down the gun barrel, see if it was clean, and it went off beside your head? Just missed your squash. You couldn't hear outta that ear for . . ."

"Shuddup, Dumwood. I ain't scared of guns. That was just a malfunction in the firearm. Anyway, I like to use my brains instead of resortin' to violence."

"Don't call me that, Eddie, or you won't have any brains."

"Don't bother, Derwood," Shamrock said. "He ain't got any brains to speak of anyway."

"All right, all right, everybody," I said in frustration. "Can it, will you? This is serious."

"Is . . . is . . . is that it?" Eddie said, pointing at the case in my hand. I could see his finger shaking.

"That's it," I said, walking over to the sofa, plopping myself down beside Tammy, and resting the case upright on the floor between my legs.

Eddie scurried around the sofa so he was facing me. He looked at the case as if it held the meaning of life. And maybe for him, it did.

"Is it really four pounds, Dan?" He must have caught whatever was making Shamrock's voice quiver, because his voice quivered too, only worse.

"It's supposed to be. I haven't seen it."

"Four pounds," Eddie said. His eyes were glazed, and I didn't like the way he said the words. He reminded me of Fred C. Dobbs in *The Treasure of the Sierra Madre*. He looked like he had gold sickness just like Fred, only his gold wasn't yellow metal, it was grayish-white powder.

"Are you all right, Tammy?" I turned, looked at her. She seemed okay but nervous. Normal for these circumstances. And she seemed straight. That was good.

She nodded. I reached over, patted her hand. She gave me a forced smile.

"Amy's not here, is she?" I asked.

She shook her head. I had the feeling her voice would shake like she had the DTs. Probably why she kept quiet. But I was glad that Amy was not going to be here during the coming events, whatever they might be.

Shamrock stood near the closed front door, his feet fidgeting. We all looked and probably felt as uncomfortable as a group of revolutionaries smoking their last cigarette against the firing squad wall.

I certainly couldn't sit around until another fifteen minutes passed and the appointed time of noon arrived. I had to take my mind off the situation. "I know Sergeant Masterson has spoken to you all, but remember that I'm supposed to do most of the talking. The rest of you say nothing but chitchat."

There were nods all the way around except for Eddie who seemed a little peeved.

"What's the matter, Eddie?" I asked.

For the first time I took stock of Eddie's getup. The purple shirt was a cheap rayon that Eddie probably thought passed for fine silk. He had it unbuttoned midway on his scrawny chest. A few black curls of hair contrasted with the heavy yellow chain he wore. I say yellow instead of gold because I was sure it wasn't real. If Eddie got his hands on real gold, he'd have already sold it. His polyester white pants went well with the shirt, if you were so inclined. White patent leather shoes, with cracks, covered his large feet.

Probably his idea of what big meth dealers all looked like.

Eddie bought his drugs at street level most of the time, I knew that much. So he must have used his imagination.

Eddie cleared his throat. "Well, Dan, to tell you the truth—you don't have the experience in this line of work, not like I do."

"You're right about that, thank god," I said.

That was the wrong thing to say. I should have shot him down right then and there. He apparently took my statement as confirmation of his superior knowledge.

Eddie strutted a couple of steps, stopping in the middle of the room. Standing like he was a senator speaking to the chamber, he said, "I'll be right beside you, Dan. Anything you start to screw up on, I'll jump right in. Or maybe I should take the lead. I'll show you how this is done."

"And I'll show you how a good beating's done," Shamrock said, heading across the floor toward Eddie, who threw his arms up to cover his face and staggered backward.

I jumped up and got in front of Shamrock just as he was about to slug Eddie, all the time keeping one eye on the briefcase. "Hold it, hold it, Shamrock."

Shamrock craned his neck to see around me, glaring at Eddie. "I ain't lettin' him run the show, Dan. With that jerk-off in charge, we'll all be as dead as rotting cabbage."

I held my hands gently against my friend's chest.

"I know," I said. "Don't worry. He's *not* running this show."

I turned around, looked at Eddie. He was still cowering a bit but was trying to reverse his humiliation—now that he saw I had Shamrock under control.

"Isn't that right, Eddie? " I said. "You're going to keep your mouth shut just as Masterson said."

Eddie nodded rapidly. "Sure, sure, Dan. Whatever you say."

I retook my seat just as someone rapped on the door. If there had been any hint of footsteps coming up the stairs, our little exchange with Eddie had muffled it. All eyes went to the door.

I swallowed hard. "You better answer it, Tammy. It looks like we're on."

Chapter 38

AND ON WE WERE. Tammy opened the door, and in walked Ponzie, Georgie right behind him. Ponzie was a bit better dressed than usual—a clean red polo shirt and designer jeans. Maybe—in contrast to Eddie—this was *his* idea of a big meth dealer. Unlike Eddie, Ponzie should know.

A large brown paper shopping bag was clutched in his right hand. It looked big enough to hold $80,000, no problem.

Georgie looked as he usually did—very dangerous. Out of the ordinary for him was his nervousness. His eyes flitted around the room.

Not all that unexpected. I was tense too, even with some chemical help keeping the nervousness under control.

"Check the place out," Ponzie said to Georgie.

When the Ape finished his quick review of the adjoining rooms, he returned and stood beside Ponzie. The two thugs didn't say anything. Neither did anyone else. Tammy walked back to the sofa, sat on the opposite end from me.

Finally, I said, "You guys want to sit?"

"Yeah," Ponzie said, pointing at me. "We'll sit there."

I was antsy anyway. I couldn't have cared less if these two lovebirds wanted to hold hands, let alone sit together. I got up, taking the briefcase with me. Ponzie took my spot, and Georgie sat between him and Tammy with his shoulder against her. I could see her shaking from where I stood; I was sure Georgie could feel it.

It didn't appear that anyone was going to speak, or maybe they couldn't speak—as in Tammy's case.

After a short minute of strained silence, I said, "You want something to drink?"

"No, what we want is to do business," Ponzie said. His voice held an unusual amount of strain. He nodded at the case in my hand. "You got all the stuff?"

I nodded. "I got it. What about you? The money?"

I looked directly at the brown paper bag in his lap.

"We got it," Ponzie said as if I'd insulted him. He nodded at the case. "Open it. I wanna see the merchandise."

I didn't like getting into this quite so fast, but I had to show the goods sooner or later. I was about to open the case when Eddie became animated.

His hands moved. "Hold on one second. I think we ought to see the color of your money at the same time, Ponzie. I've been in quite a few big deals and we always . . ."

"Shuddup, ya disco duck, or I'll throw you out the window and this time it won't be open," Ponzie snarled. "You're only here cause . . ."

He hesitated as if he'd almost said something he shouldn't. He turned to Derwood, still sitting in the easy chair. "How about you? Anything to say?"

Derwood gulped and shook his head.

It was odd seeing a big guy like Derwood terrified. It amped up my own uneasiness.

"And you, Irishman?" Ponzie said.

"Not right now," Shamrock said meekly.

Ponzie grunted.

"I hope that brings us all luck," he said, pointing at the design on Shamrock's sweatshirt.

"Let's see it," Ponzie said, getting back to business.

I walked over to the coffee table in front of the couch, released the two clasps on the case, opened it, and carefully turned the case towards Ponzie.

"Put it down," he said. "So I can get a good look at it."

I set the case gently on the table. There were four large sealed zip-lock bags. Each was stuffed with a grayish-white powder. Ponzie poked the bags with his finger. You couldn't tell much that way, which he knew—of course.

He looked at me. "I'm going to take a taste."

He wasn't asking, he was telling, so I didn't say anything. He pulled out one of the ziplock bags, closed the case, and set the plastic bag on it. Just as he was starting to pull the bag open, Eddie piped up.

"You better have me try that for you, Ponz." He tapped his chest. "I'm quite an expert in this field."

I looked daggers at Eddie. The fool was trying to ingratiate himself with a big meth dealer. Apparently, he believed that would benefit his little habit in the future. He'd obviously become so mesmerized by the sight of all the meth, he'd forgotten that these two dealers were on a one-way ride to the state prison for a decade or more. Unless the dolt wanted a jolt that bad.

Whatever the reason, I hoped it wouldn't upend our sting.

"Don't ya remember what I said about the window, Hoar?" Ponzie snapped. "Pick a pane or shut up."

"Sure, Ponzie, sure. Whatever you say," Eddie said, backing away.

Ponzie opened the ziplock. He wet his finger with his tongue and dipped the wet finger into the powder. A small amount of the gray-tinged drug stuck to the wet finger as he brought it to his mouth and tasted it gingerly with his tongue. He made a face like he'd tasted something bitter.

That was a good sign, but apparently it wasn't enough for Ponzie. He removed a small jackknife from his jean's pocket and opened the blade.

Ponzie was about to give this product the definitive test—unless you had a chemist with you. And Georgie was no chemist. I could only hope that the stuff Masterson had acquired for the sting was the real McCoy, otherwise there'd be big trouble.

I held my breath as Ponzie slid the small blade into the bag and removed a little pile of the powder. He brought the knife up to his right nostril and inhaled deeply.

I thought his head was going to pop off or spin around at least. His eyes dilated like a camera lens. His head shook and the shaking snaked down the upper half of his body.

When he was done with the shivers, I was surprised to see Ponzie dig his knife back into the bag of meth and pull out another mound. But instead of doing it himself, and maybe becoming more dangerous than he already was, he turned to the Ape. "Try this. It's real good."

Ponzie leaned over and assisted Georgie in a repeat of the nose hoovering that Ponzie had just done. I didn't like the look on Georgie's face one bit. Reminded me of a wanted poster featuring an escapee from the Bridgewater Prison for the Criminally Insane.

I was having heart palpitations all of a sudden. If I didn't get this nightmare over soon, I might not be able to complete it. "Can I see the money now?"

Unlike Ponzie I'd asked, not demanded. I was somewhat relieved when he smiled and said, "Sure, kid, here it is."

He put his knife away, sealed the ziplock, then closed and secured the briefcase. He opened the brown paper bag in his lap and reached in.

His hand came out holding a dark .357 magnum. He pointed it at me and said, "Don't anyone make a fuckin' move."

All I could do was stare down the barrel of a gun that looked as wide as a train tunnel and wonder, now what?

Chapter 39

"WHERE'S THE PHONE?" Ponzie growled. He leaned forward and glared at Tammy huddled on the far side of the Ape.

"Kitchen," she answered.

"Beep him." Ponzie nodded at Georgie.

Georgie the Ape got up from the sofa and went to the kitchen.

"You and you, up," Ponzie said to Tammy and Derwood.

After they stood, Ponzie got up and used his gun to herd us close to a wall. "Everyone stand over there."

"You too, Hoar," Ponzie added, turning the gun toward Eddie—who had been slowly sidestepping toward the kitchen. "You ain't going nowhere."

Eddie hustled over. "Look, P . . . P . . . Ponzie. I ain't got nothing to do with that stuff."

He pointed at the attaché case on the table. "You can take it all. I won't squeal. I'm stand-up. You know me."

Ponzie harrumphed. "Yeah, I know you, Hoar. That's why you gotta go."

I had an idea what that meant, and I didn't like it. If they were planning on killing Eddie, then we all were going to die.

Eddie's head began to shake. "But, Ponzie, please, I'll never say anything." He looked as desperate as a man could. "I'll . . . I'll even help you get rid of the bodies. I can get a boat from the harbor. Yeah . . . yeah, that's the ticket. I know someone who . . ."

Shamrock shoved me out of the way and was on Eddie before anyone could stop him. His right fist connected with the side of Eddie's head. Eddie howled, threw his hands to his face, and staggered backward. Shamrock followed with a volley of punches that didn't seem like they did much damage. Eddie hunched over, arms protecting his face, and Shamrock's punches, though hard, couldn't get past the arms.

I didn't move. Neither did anyone else. Ponzie chuckled for a minute. When he got bored watching Shamrock whale on Eddie, he moved close and poked Shamrock in the head with the barrel end of the big gun,

"Okay, Red," Ponzie said. "Knock it off."

Shamrock lowered his fists to his sides, breathing heavily. "You squirmy serpent," he snarled at Eddie. "I'd like to plant you head first in a bog!"

Eddie slowly stood up and lowered his arms. There was a welt on the side of his face. He wore an expression that was a weird cross between humiliation, fear, and pain.

He was lucky. If Shamrock's punch had connected with his jaw, I had no doubt that Eddie would be drinking through a straw for at least a month—*if* he lived that long.

"Eddie, you were gonna help kill them?" Derwood said as if it was impossible to believe. "And me too?"

Eddie rubbed the side of his face gingerly. "Ahh, I was only faking, Dumwood. You know me, I'd never do that. I was . . . ahh . . . just looking for a way out. Yeah, that's it. I was lookin' for a way out. For all of us."

He smiled, then appeared to remember Ponzie was still around and holding a gun.

Eddie turned to the big man. "Look, Ponzie, I didn't mean—"

"Shuddup, ya slimy rat," Ponzie roared. He lowered his voice and gave Eddie a wicked smirk. "Maybe I better do you first. What do you think?"

Eddie looked like he was literally shitting his pants. "P . . . P . . . P . . . Ponz, no, please."

Ponzie laughed. "Get the fuck over there with the others before I smack you in the head with this." He jiggled the huge gun in his hand.

Eddie moved like a rocket to my side. Shamrock returned to the group, too.

Georgie came back into the room and nodded.

"We got a short wait," Ponzie said. "Don't anyone move while we're waiting. Or we'll kill you now."

My brain started spinning like a carousel gone wild. They *were* going to kill us. Where in the hell was Masterson? Would he be in time? I judged the distance to Ponzie and his gun, but I didn't think he was close enough that I could get to him before he blew a hole in my gut as big as a baseball.

If I could clue them in somehow, I knew I could rely on Shamrock and maybe even Derwood to help rush Ponzie if things got that desperate. I didn't want to endanger Tammy, and Eddie would be no help.

At least one of us was sure to die in such an attempt and there was no guarantee of success.

I decided to wait until the last possible moment. Any second, Masterson could crash though the door with the cavalry before there was need for a suicide mission.

Tammy grabbed my hand, squeezed it. She was standing beside me, silent. I could feel her hand shaking and her palm was damp with sweat.

Or was it me? Maybe I was the one shaking and sweating.

At this point, it mattered little.

I hoped whoever we were waiting for had a case of diarrhea and was delayed. Time was our friend after all. The longer we waited, the more likely Masterson and his men would burst in.

In fact, I wondered why he hadn't showed up already.

We all stood there. Ponzie, with his gun, and Georgie with those wild eyes.

Eddie opened his mouth. Started to speak. Ponzie threatened to shoot out his teeth one by one. Eddie clammed up.

Footsteps thudded on the porch and all eyes went to the door. I was hopeful it was our rescue. There was a light tap from the other side.

"He's here," Ponzie said to the Ape. "Let him in."

Georgie walked to the door, flipped the deadbolt, and opened it.

Chapter 40

SERGEANT MIKEY FERGUSON stood in the doorway for a moment. He closed the door, lumbered in and stood beside Ponzie.

Ferguson wore a nasty smirk on his ugly face. The smirk widened when he said, "Surprised, Marlowe?"

"Not one bit," I said. "I expected it."

Those words wiped the smirk off Ferguson's face. "I had the feeling that might be how you felt. Now you got me doing something I don't like."

"Then don't do it," I shot back.

Tammy squeezed my hand tight. She probably didn't like me antagonizing Ferguson. I just had to keep him talking until Masterson showed up.

The door knob turned again. The door opened—speak of the devil.

Massachusetts State cop Jack Masterson hustled in. He slammed the door behind him.

My brain spun like a pinwheel as I realized Masterson was alone. His hands were at his sides instead of holding a gun.

Looked like my attorney had been right not to trust Masterson. Also explained my nagging doubts about all this—in part.

The son-of-a-bitch was in on the deal!

Shamrock said, "What the fuck?"

"Oh, momma," Eddie whimpered.

I was scared but I was pissed too. "You're crooked, Masterson? You're in with them?"

He didn't answer, but Ferguson said, "You didn't think I could get away with all I been doing for years without some state help, did you, Marlowe?"

When I didn't answer, he continued. "For a guy who's supposedly been around you're not too smart. You knew about a reverse sting operation but fell like a dead tree for a double reverse sting. Now we got you all here at once, just like we wanted."

"Hey, hey," Masterson said. "Don't be telling him anything."

Ferguson let out an evil little chuckle. "It doesn't make any difference now."

Masterson grumbled, then said, "Let's just do what we gotta do and get out of here."

"I won't talk," Eddie said hysterically. "I . . . I'll do whatever you say. I . . . I . . . I'll even say I did it. Yeah, I did it. I killed them. I'll keep my mouth shut and do the time. Sure, they'll buy me doin' the murders."

"You fuckin' rat," Ponzie said. He held his gun on us and maintained a safe distance.

"Go smack him for me, will ya?" he said to Georgie.

The Ape jostled his way between us and hit Eddie with a right cross that floored the skinny man even though he had his arms protecting his head. Then Georgie shoved his way back to Ponzie's side.

Eddie moaned and sat up, rubbing his face. He didn't look good. He made no effort to stand.

"Can I do that?" Shamrock said.

"Shut up, mick," Ferguson said. "Don't get smart."

"Come on, let's get this over with," Masterson said impatiently.

"Hold your horses, will you," Ferguson said. "We got to take our time. There can't be no screwups here."

He looked at Tammy. "You got anything to drink?"

"Juice," Tammy answered.

"Get us some." He turned to Georgie. "Watch her. I don't want her bolting out the back door."

Tammy walked into the kitchen. Georgie followed her but stopped at the doorway where he could see into the kitchen and still keep an eye on us.

Ferguson put on a sly grin. "You know, Eddie, that's a good idea. You takin' the blame and all."

Eddie struggled to his feet, tripped, regained his balance. "Sure, sure. I always got good ideas."

Another red welt had sprouted on Eddie's face.

"Too bad we already thought of it," Ferguson said. "But don't worry, Eddie. You won't have to do any time."

Eddie moaned. It was an awful sound.

"Cut the crap," Masterson said. "We've got work to do."

"Yeah, we do." Ferguson nodded. He removed a gun from under his coat at the back of his waistband—a long-barreled .22. I didn't know a lot about guns, but I *had* seen a long-barreled .22 before. I'd even fired one or two over at the shooting range.

Ferguson removed a metal cylindrical object from his coat pocket and proceeded to screw it onto the pistol's barrel.

My stomach sank. That had to be a silencer, or suppressor, or whatever the hell it was called.

"Oh, Jesus, please no," Eddie said with a pitiful whimper.

Tammy returned from the kitchen with three glasses of juice held between two hands. She set them on the coffee table, came back to my side, and held my hand.

"Dan, please . . ." Tammy said. She squeezed so hard I could almost hear my bones breaking. Tears streamed down her cheeks.

I squeezed her hand back.

I'd gotten her into this. I'd gotten all of us into it—me, Tammy, Shamrock, Derwood, yeah, even Eddie. I couldn't blame Eddie for his actions any more than I could blame Tammy for her tears.

I should have seen this coming. I glanced at the briefcase on the table. For all I knew that wasn't even meth. That would explain Ponzie having no qualms about sampling the powder back at his pawnshop and here. Georgie, too. If so, they were good actors. Still, I should have seen through Masterson and his cockamamie story.

But I hadn't.

And now I was going to pay.

Unfortunately, the others were going to pay too. Only one good side—they wouldn't suffer for much longer. And I wouldn't be feeling guilty for any more time than it took Ferguson to get that killing instrument ready.

Thoughts of my children flooded my mind, almost overwhelming me. I had to force those thoughts out. If I didn't, I might miss a chance to turn the tables.

Or I'd crack up.

Or both.

Ferguson had secured the suppressor and checked to make sure the gun was loaded. "Okay."

"C . . . can I have a glass of juice?" Eddie looked like he was actually squirming in his skin.

"Fuck you," Ferguson growled.

"You want him to do it?" Ponzie asked, nodding toward Georgie.

"That's what I was thinking," Ferguson said. "But not with that. Too loud." He frowned at the magnum in Ponzie's hand.

"You okay with doing the heavy work?" Ferguson moved his gaze to Georgie, who just nodded.

"You, mick, on the floor," Ferguson said.

I looked over my shoulder. There was no rosy cast to Shamrock's face now; it was as white as flour.

"Move! Now! Lie on your back."

Derwood took a couple of steps to give Shamrock room to follow orders, which he did, slowly lying down on the floor and stretching out.

I burped up bile as I watched my friend. My brain had gone completely blank.

"You, bitch, get down beside him," Ferguson said to Tammy. A pitiful little sound came from her throat, but she didn't move.

Ferguson took a couple of steps and holding the gun on me, he grabbed Tammy's free hand and tugged. She didn't go anywhere. I don't know if she was still holding tight, but I sure was. I wasn't letting her go anywhere.

Ferguson glared at me.

"Keep your gun on him, Ponzie," he said. He shifted the .22 from me, swinging the end of the barrel so it made contact with the front of Tammy's forehead.

The hand I held was shaking so hard I could feel my whole arm vibrating.

"Let go, Marlowe," Ferguson said. "Or I'll do her right here."

I believed him. So did she. Our grips loosened and our hands dropped.

"Get the fuck down beside him," Ferguson growled. Tammy stretched out on her back, just like Shamrock beside her.

"You won't get away with this, Ferguson," I said. "You either, Masterson. They'll know it was you. How can you explain five dead bodies?"

I was pretty sure I knew the answer to that, but I wanted to keep them talking. Stall for time. Why? Because stall is what you do when you're about ready to die. Try it sometime, you'll see.

"Oh, we will, Marlowe," Ferguson said. "Eddie had the right idea. What we have here is a little meth deal between you, the Irishman, and the broad on one side, and the two jerk-offs on the other side. But . . . kinda sad . . . something went wrong. A rip-off. Eddie and his buddy executed the two on the floor. And you . . . well, you were beside them. But Eddie ain't too bright, as we all know, and you had a gun hidden on you. You made a move just as Eddie was ready to give you a slug in the head. You opened up and when the smoke cleared, you'd killed both Eddie and Derwood. Unfortunately, one of their bullets killed you, too. See, smart ass? See what happens to all these nice people just because you nosed around, finding out things you shouldn't have. They're all dying because of you, jackass, and you're forcing us to do it. And the kicker is that stuff ain't nothing but cut. And no one came with any money. You were going to rip each other off." He let out a sick little chuckle.

So I'd been right about the meth being fake, for the good it did. "You're dreaming, Ferguson," I said. My voice shook. "I haven't got any gun. And I never carry one."

"That's where you're wrong, Marlowe." Ferguson looked at Masterson. "Show him."

Masterson pulled his sport coat aside and removed a gun from his waistband. He pointed it in our direction.

"Recognize it, Marlowe?" Ferguson asked before he let out a short laugh.

I couldn't be sure from this distance, but Ferguson had given enough of a hint for me to realize the .38 caliber pistol in Masterson's hand *was* probably mine.

"You shouldn't have left it in your nightstand," Ferguson said. "Made it too easy to get when Georgie paid a visit to your cottage when you were out poking around . You'll be found holding this with some slugs from it in the two twerps. And Eddie there? Well, we'll plant the .22 on him. I got another throwaway we can gift to . . . what is it? Derwood? Dumwood? Whatever, that's how it's going down."

"Cut the talk," Masterson said angrily. "Let's do it and get the hell out of here."

"All right, all right," Ferguson said. He held out the .22.

"You're doing the honors," he told Georgie.

Georgie lumbered over, took the .22 from Ferguson's hand.

"Do the girl first," Ferguson said.

Georgie grunted, walked over to where Shamrock and Tammy lay prone on the floor.

I had to make a move, but I couldn't. Not only was Ponzie pointing the magnum dead at me, Masterson had my own gun pointed at me. They must have both thought that if anyone was going to make a last ditch move, it would be me. Looking around at Eddie and Derwood standing over to the side, I knew they were right. If there was any doubt I ever had about the term *frozen with fear*, it went out the window right then and there. Eddie and Derwood might as well have been mannequins for all the help they'd be.

And Shamrock was on the floor.

I was on my own with two guns pointed dead center at me. A feeling of hopelessness rushed over me like the ocean at high tide.

Georgie leaned down, pointed the barrel of the .22 at Tammy's right eye. She sobbed and I turned my head away. I felt like I was going to be ill.

"Watch out for the backsplash," Ferguson said to Georgie.

Chapter 41

I'D LIKE TO say I suddenly turned hero, found unexpected courage and took down the bad guys. I didn't. I'd given up.

Until the noise started.

"This is the Hampton Police. We've got the house surrounded."

A bull horn or so I assumed. And it came from the street. Even though it was somewhat muffled, I recognized the voice.

Lieutenant Richard Gant.

And was I happy, for once, to hear his voice.

Looked like my "insurance policy" was about to pay off.

James Connolly had put some doubt in my mind about whether I could fully trust Masterson. So when James did call me back, as he promised, we made a plan for him to get in touch with Steve Moore. Run what Masterson had proposed by him. See what Steve thought. Obviously, James had followed through. I'd wondered when I hadn't heard from either one of them.

Georgie jumped up from his crouched position over Tammy. "Whadda we do? Whadda we do?" he said almost hysterically.

"Shut up, you fool," Ferguson said, pulling his police gun from its holster. "Let me think." He grabbed a glass of juice off the table and drank it.

"Come out, one at a time, with your hands raised." Gant again.

I glanced at Shamrock on the floor. He looked up at me and nodded, his lips tight. He must have seen the same glimmer of hope on my face that I could see on his. Tammy was also still on the floor. She lifted her head and gave me a forced little smile. I returned it.

Derwood was a wooden Indian, and Eddie, well, for once, Eddie kept his mouth shut. Probably didn't want to draw attention to himself, what with the large stain around his crotch area.

Georgie the Ape just stood there, gun in hand. He was too stupid to know what to do without one of the others telling him.

Masterson looked from the door to the gun in his hand and back again, probably wondering how the hell he ever got in this position.

Ponzie hadn't moved. He still held his piece pointed in my direction, but occasionally he'd glance nervously at Ferguson. He could probably see the wheels spinning in Ferguson's mind just as I could.

And Ferguson? He was calculating how he could get out of here in one piece. He didn't care about anyone else. I had a feeling he'd kill everyone in the room if there had been a scintilla of a possibility that he could get away with it.

Fortunately, there wasn't.

There were eight others, including his buddies. He'd have to kill them too if he wanted no witnesses left. And all three of them were armed.

Besides, the cops out front would probably rush the door the second anyone started shooting.

Ferguson stayed silent until finally he looked toward the kitchen.

"We'll try the back door," he said. "Georgie, you go first. Wait for us at the cars. You know where we left 'em, right."

Georgie looked at Ferguson as if he'd suddenly grown a second head. "Yeah, but what if they're out there waitin' for us?"

Guess Georgie wasn't as dumb as I'd thought.

"They aren't out there," Ferguson shot back. "Not out back. This town is lucky they got enough cops to cover the front."

"Yeah, but they might be," Georgie said. He sounded tentative, as if he wasn't used to questioning an order.

"Oh, for Chrissake, you pussy," Ferguson said mockingly. "Even if there are one or two cops out back, they're just summer cops, kids. Fire a couple rounds, they'll scatter."

Georgie grumbled something, then reverted to stupid again. With his gun in his hand, he disappeared into the kitchen. Ferguson and Masterson shared a glance. They'd know soon if they had a chance of getting out that way.

It didn't take long. I knew as soon as Georgie stepped through the back door. Shouts were followed by two quick pistol shots and the loud boom of what was most likely a shotgun.

Masterson raced to the kitchen. In half a minute he was back.

"I locked the door. We aren't getting out that way," was all he said.

"Maybe we better give up," Ponzie said.

"Maybe he's right," Masterson said. "I can . . . I mean we can beat this."

"Are you shitting me?" Ferguson roared. "They've most likely got me tied to Mariani's murder. You too! And who knows what else they'll want to hang on us."

His eyes narrowed as he looked at me. "Imagine what these assholes are going to testify to. They've heard enough to make it all stick."

"Yeah, but I ain't gonna die here like this." Ponzie was almost shrieking now. "I'll get a good lawyer."

He dropped his gun on the floor and headed for the front door. He opened the door a crack and shouted, "I'm coming out."

Ferguson moved faster than I would expect from a man his size. Just as Ponzie opened the door wide enough to squeeze out, Ferguson gave Ponzie a hard push, shoving him through the doorway. As soon as Ponzie disappeared onto the porch, Ferguson poked his gun outside and let off a shot, then slammed the door.

A split second later I heard Ponzie scream, "Don't shoot. Please don't—"

A volley of gunshots erupted. Ferguson was already ducking behind the sofa. Those of us still standing dropped to the floor. No one wanted to get hit by a stray shot.

And no one inside did, although we all knew that Ponzie would no longer be pawning hot jewelry.

"What now?" Masterson shouted to Ferguson. "We give up, take a chance?"

Ferguson's ugly face peeked over the couch. "We ain't got no chance that way. We give up, there'll be no bail, and there's no way we can beat this in court. We'll be *in* for life."

"What then?" Masterson asked. "We can't get out the front or the back."

He grabbed a glass of juice off the coffee table and gulped it.

Ferguson pointed his pistol over the sofa at Tammy.

"That's your car in the driveway, right?" Ferguson asked.

Tammy didn't answer. One look at her face told me why. Sheer terror.

"Bitch," Ferguson shouted. "That's your car, right?"

"Yeah . . . yeah," Tammy managed.

"Where are the keys?" Ferguson demanded.

"The kitch . . . the kitchen. On the hook."

"Good," Ferguson said as if his plan had already succeeded. "That's how we're getting out of here."

"That won't work," Masterson said. "You saw what happened to Georgie. We won't even make it to the car."

"Her car is right there by the back stairs, you stupid shit," Ferguson bellowed. "Besides, we'll take two of them with us. They won't shoot them."

"I dunno . . ." Masterson said. I could tell he was mulling over his chances of making a break for it or just giving up.

"You better know," Ferguson roared. "I told you this day might come. I told you to stash dough around the country, just in case. I did. Didn't you?"

"Yeah, but—"

"But nothing. It's either the car or Concord for life. Imagine how that'd be for us? Two ex-cops. You'd be the sweetheart of some muscle-bound punk within a week."

Masterson seemed to be mulling that over. He didn't speak and after a minute, when he still hadn't said anything, Ferguson took the silence as acceptance of his idea.

I did, too.

Ferguson struggled up from behind the sofa, walked over to the door. He kept his huge body to one side of the door and opened it a crack.

"Listen," he shouted. "We're going out the back and taking the car. Don't try to stop us or follow us. If you do, we'll kill them all."

Ferguson waited a short time. There was no response from outside.

"Tell the kids out back to hold their fire," he continued. "Otherwise someone out there's gonna take the heat for a whole bunch of innocent dead people."

Ferguson closed the door and came back. "Okay, we're taking two with us."

"Who," Masterson asked, standing again.

"The broad. Who else? They won't shoot a woman."

"You want to bet?" Masterson said.

"Believe me," Ferguson said. "I been working with jerks like this for thirty years. They won't shoot anyway. They'll be too scared they'd be the ones charged with murder."

"You. Get up," Ferguson said loudly, grabbing Tammy by the arm and pulling her roughly to her feet.

"And you," Ferguson added, nodding in my direction.

I was on the floor, like most of us had been since the gunfire erupted. I stood up unassisted.

Ferguson ordered Eddie and Derwood to move from the floor and get over beside Shamrock. They both hurried into position, lying back down next to Shamrock.

For some reason, Shamrock stood up. Maybe he'd just had enough. I don't know. Ferguson took a step toward Shamrock and whacked him on the back of the head with the pistol. Shamrock crumpled into a fetal position on the floor and lay there—unmoving.

I lunged at Ferguson but stopped when he turned the gun on me.

"For the best, Marlowe," Ferguson said. "The mick was the only one that might have followed us out." Glancing at Eddie and Derwood on the floor, he added, "You boys won't be moving until we're out of the state, will you?"

"No, sir," Eddie said as if he were talking to the nicest person on Earth.

I frowned but I expected no less from Eddie. And I had to give Ferguson one thing—he was a good judge of people. Shamrock might have made a play if he'd thought that Tammy and I were going to our deaths.

Derwood would do whatever Eddie told him and that would be not to move until the car was somewhere near Boston.

"If we're going, let's go," Masterson said.

"Move," Fergusson said, waving his gun in the general direction of the kitchen.

Tammy led the way and I followed. Masterson followed me with Ferguson bringing up the rear.

We quickly crossed the small kitchen, Ferguson grabbing the keys on the way. We reached the door leading to the back and her car in the driveway.

What was to happen next . . . I had no idea. All I could hope was that Tammy and I would live through it.

Chapter 42

ONCE OUTSIDE, WE walked single file down the back steps. First Tammy, then Ferguson, me, and Masterson, in that order. Masterson had a grip on the collar of my shirt. He stumbled on the last step, going to his knees, and dragging my collar with him.

"Get up you idiot," Ferguson hissed over his shoulder.

Masterson struggled to his feet and used his gun to nudge me toward the old beat-up Ford Escort.

"I'm driving," Ferguson said. He used Tammy as a shield as he worked his way to the driver's side. He opened both doors and forced Tammy in back while he maneuvered his big frame into the driver's seat. While this was going on, Masterson did the same on the other side of the car, using me for his shield.

In the back seat, Tammy slid over close to me. She didn't seem quite as terrified as she had earlier. Masterson, who was in the front passenger seat, rested the gun on the top of the seat and pointed it at me. He had a strange glaze in his eyes.

Ferguson started the car, and we moved slowly down the short driveway to the street.

Hampton cruisers, some with lights flashing, were parked every which way. Cops were behind most of the cruisers, leaning over hoods and trunks, pointing guns—mostly pistols—but there were at least a couple with shotguns.

My heart raced as I prayed they'd hold their fire. If they didn't, I feared Tammy's car would look like Bonnie and Clyde's after their final day on earth.

Ferguson pulled out onto the street and maneuvered around the police cars. As we drove the short distance to Ashworth Avenue, I got a glimpse of Gant, still holding the bullhorn, behind an unmarked car. Steve Moore was standing beside him. Steve's face reminded me of someone watching a funeral procession passing. I hoped that wasn't an omen.

At the corner of Ashworth Avenue, a large group of people were lined up on the opposite side of the street, trying to get a look at the action. A few patrolmen kept them from getting any closer. When we turned onto Ashworth, Ferguson drove the few streets to the turn-around for Ocean Boulevard but didn't take it. I hadn't thought he would. It was a fairly nice day. The sun was out and it was warm and he would've been sure to get caught up in traffic on the main drag.

Instead, he headed straight for the bridge that led to Seabrook. There weren't many cars going that way . . . yet. That would happen later in the afternoon when the day-trippers left the beach.

Now, though, we had clear sailing over the Hampton Bridge. I took a glance at the nuclear power plant on my right. The sun bounced off the dome. For once, I hoped I'd see that ugly sight again.

Tammy nudged me with her elbow. I looked. She partially blocked her mouth with one hand and tried to mouth something, but I could only make out one word—tranquilizers.

"Knock it off," Masterson said, his words oddly thick. Now his eyes seemed out of focus rather than just glazed.

We'd just about reached the turn for Route 286—which leads to interstate 95 and could take us just about anywhere. I was sure Ferguson would go that way.

Sure enough, Ferguson took the 286 option.

Just as we took the turn, Masterson's head dropped on the top of the seat, his eyes closed. His gun hand had disappeared somewhere down on the seat beside him.

Finally, I understood what Tammy had been trying to tell me—she'd Mickey'd their drinks.

Of course, Ferguson noticed. "What the fuck's the matter with you?"

He fished for Masterson's weapon on the seat beside him.

I didn't wait for him to snag his fish.

I lunged to the other side of the car, reaching for Ferguson's neck. I was almost sitting in Tammy's lap now. Ferguson grabbed the gun from the seat, bobbled it. The gun fell to the floor and Ferguson leaned forward to reach it. I followed him, forcing both of my arms under his armpits. Then I lifted his weight as best I could and pulled the big man toward me until I could lock the fingers of my hands together behind his neck in as close to the old "full nelson" as I could get. I leaned back, pulled, and squeezed as hard as I could.

Ferguson must have instinctively floored the gas pedal because the car roared ahead.

"Stop the car, Ferguson," I screamed. "Stop the car."

Tammy screamed, too.

The car didn't slow down.

Cars littered the road ahead of us along with people crossing the street to get to one of two fried food joints that were opposite each other.

It took only a moment to realize we were on a collision course with Brown's, the restaurant on this side of the street. The restaurant was a landmark, packed every summer day.

Still holding Ferguson in the full nelson, I half-stood, shoving his head forward. I hit the horn with my elbow and let the horn blare. People and cars scattered everywhere.

Ferguson gurgled something. I couldn't make it out.

A couple with two kids who'd been trying to cross the street from Brown's were suddenly in front of us, frozen like deer in a headlight. We were going to plow right into them—unless I did something.

I had only two choices, and I didn't like either of them. I let go of Ferguson's neck with my left hand, grabbed the steering wheel, and turned hard to the left. Our car swerved across the opposite lane, flew through a small part of Markey's Restaurant lot, and slammed into, and through, a two-foot high metal guardrail.

Ferguson was torn from my arm, and his head made a sickening thud against the steering wheel. Tammy flew partially into the front seat. I had the sensation we were airborne. And then the car violently shuddered as we landed. My body flew upward, my head slamming hard against the roof.

A bright red eruption filled my head. I watched the exploding lights in fascination until a black curtain dropped swiftly down.

Then, either a minute or a year later, I was in cold water. It felt so good, I didn't mind . . .

Until the water reached my mouth and I started spitting it out almost as fast as it came in.

Too fast.

Someone grabbed me, pulling my head out of the water. I struggled, but whoever had me was too strong, so I gave up. I could hear voices now, shouts. The grinding of metal—car doors being forced open?

The arms that had grabbed me were pulling me free of the car.

Then I was being towed head first—on my back—through the water.

I twisted my upper body, tried to see what was happening. Gant and Steve Moore each had one of my arms and they were pulling me along like two kids with a boogie board.

It was a nice dream.

Such a nice dream I didn't want to wake up.

Epilogue

LUCKILY, I DID wake up. In Exeter Hospital.

What had happened hadn't been a dream at all. Steve Moore and Lieutenant Gant had saved my life. Not just mine—Tammy's, too.

Unfortunately for Ferguson, by the time they got him free—after too much time spent struggling with his large girth—it was too late. He died in the ambulance.

Masterson's passenger door had been jammed, so he'd had to wait until they removed Ferguson to get to him. Because of that delay, he hadn't stood a chance. He hadn't regained consciousness, as far as I knew.

At least, that's the way the story was told to me—lying in that hospital bed.

On either side of me, sitting in chairs they'd pulled close, were my best friend and one of the men who had saved my life.

"How's your head," I asked Shamrock, referring to the whack he'd taken from Ferguson's gun.

"Just a lump," he answered. "I have a very hard head."

"And Tammy's all right?" I asked.

"She's fine, Danny," Shamrock said, his face beaming. His skin was back to a healthy rose color. "They didn't even keep the lassie overnight. Touched up a few minor dings and off she went."

"How'd she seem otherwise?" I asked warily.

"She probably went to get a shot," Steve said.

"Maybe not," I responded. "After all that's happened, and what could've happened to her daughter, it might be enough to—"

"Once a junkie, always a junkie," Steve said.

"I don't believe that, Steve," I said. Then, not wanting to start a silly argument with the man who had just saved my life, I quickly added, "If it weren't for her, who knows what would've happened."

Steve shrugged grudgingly.

"We're going to have to help her, Shamrock, after what she did for us. Maybe we can get her a job, help her with her daughter, get her clean if we can. We owe her."

"Aye, Danny. We'll help her. Don't worry." Shamrock was dead serious.

"If there's anything I can do, you can count on me, too," Steve added.

That made me feel better. Steve's offer especially.

"I know that, Steve," I said.

"That was a great idea of hers, serving those drinks with the knockout drops," Shamrock said with a smile. He probably didn't like the somber mood the conversation was taking.

Thinking about Tammy's brilliant move did brighten me up. "You mean the tranquilizers?"

Shamrock nodded.

"Says she'd just gotten a legal scrip for them the day before," Steve said. "Crushed them up and put an elephant-size dose in all three drinks she served. That big ape was either too stupid or distracted to notice."

"What about Ferguson?" I asked. "How come he didn't pass out? He drank one, I think."

"Yeah. That's what Tammy told me," Steve said. "But it probably would take a lot longer for the drug to hit a fat slob like that."

"It's probably just kicking in now," I said. "Too bad he's not around to enjoy the relaxation."

We all had a good laugh. Then I remembered something. "Wait a minute. Tammy served three drinks. What happened to the third one?"

Shamrock and Steve both burst out laughing. I looked from one to the other, let them go on until I couldn't take it anymore, "Okay, okay. What happened to it?"

Steve tried to get his laughter under control. "That's the best part . . . the third drink went . . ."

He began laughing again.

"You tell him." He pointed at Shamrock.

Shamrock, who was used to relating the funniest of tales with a straight face, began the story. But I could see even he was struggling to get it out. "It was . . . it was . . . it was Eddie, the arse. He snuck the third glass even after Ferguson told him to keep his hands off it. Stupid shit-for-brains."

Steve was getting a handle on his laughter. "When the police finally got in there, they found him passed out and curled up in the fireplace. They had to rush him to the hospital."

"Is he all right?" I asked, assuming he was by the way they were acting like two hyenas. The laughter stopped.

"Ahh, yeah, he's okay," Shamrock said.

I waited a heartbeat, then finally asked the question that had been bothering me since Gant hollered over the bullhorn. "Why the hell did you and Gant and the cavalry show up at Tammy's house anyway, Steve? I know James talked to you, but I didn't think anyone—especially Gant—would believe him."

Steve frowned. "I had a feeling about Masterson. I didn't know him that well. Bill Walkowski pointed me in his direction, said he knew him from some regional drug task force they'd been on together."

He stopped, looked at me like he was waiting for an objection. When he didn't get one, he continued. "I was worried about you, especially since I put you in contact with Masterson. I called in a favor over in Salisbury. Someone told me they'd heard a rumor that Ferguson and Masterson may have been tight. So I started the ball rolling. Then I heard from your lawyer, Connolly. He told me both he and you weren't a hundred percent sure of Masterson. He let me know when the deal was going down. That was all I had to hear. I was able to convince Gant that there was something going on between Masterson and Ferguson. That the *something* had to do with Sal Mariani's murder and that we should put a team on this supposed drug deal. He agreed."

"Did he also agree that Shamrock and I weren't the murderers?" I asked.

Steve snorted. "That was the hard part. Especially concerning you. Gant doesn't like you."

"That goes without saying," I said.

"But I think he knew deep down that it wasn't you. He's got good cop instincts. That's why he bought my theory that Masterson was mixed up with Ferguson." He hesitated. "Well, that, and what a couple of informants told us."

"Who?" I asked.

Steve shook his head. "You know I can't tell you that, Dan."

I accepted that. Then I remembered something else. "The car that followed me when I was headed for Joe's Meat Shoppe to see Masterson, the one I couldn't read the plate number. That was *you*!"

Steve smiled sheepishly. "We had you under surveillance for a while. You were possibly in danger, so we kept a close eye on you."

"But wait a second . . ." I said. "What if Ferguson and Masterson actually *had* killed me . . . or all of us? You were taking quite a chance with our lives."

Steve looked troubled. "Like I said, we had you under surveillance. A lot."

He talked quickly. "I wasn't going to let anything happen to you. Or Shamrock. Or anyone. Look how it turned out."

"Mmm," I said doubtfully.

"And when I came in here today, you *did* say I saved your life," Steve said, looking embarrassed.

"You did."

"And Gant did, too."

I didn't like thinking about that. "What about Selma and the guy with the glasses?"

"The pawnshop's been raided," Steve said. "They confiscated a lot of stolen goods and some dope. So, Selma—and everyone else connected with the shop—will do time. And the government will probably seize the place."

"Who was that guy with the thick glasses anyway?" I asked.

"Just some cheap shyster that Ferguson and Ponzie used," Steve answered. "He'd be disbarred, except that he already is."

"What about the firebombing at Shamrock's?" I asked.

Steve shrugged. "Most likely Ponzie just got carried away and hired some kid hoping to scare you both. Probably didn't run it by Ferguson first."

I couldn't think of anything else to ask, so Steve said, "Has Dianne been here?"

"Nope," I answered.

Shamrock shifted uncomfortably in his chair as I asked cautiously, "Has she said anything?"

"She asked how you were," Shamrock said. Then, forcing a positive tone, he continued, "She's asked me more than once, Danny. She surely has."

"Mmm," was all I said.

"How about the kids?" Steve asked, probably wanting to get off the Dianne subject. "They been here?"

He was asking about the two children from my first and only marriage, Dave and Jess. I told him and Shamrock about the great visit I had from them a couple of hours previous. That changed the mood to upbeat for a while.

When we'd said about as much as we could on that subject, Shamrock asked, "They say how long you going to be here, Danny?"

"A few more days, I guess. But I don't see why. I'm not feeling that bad."

"You almost died, for Chrissake," Steve said. "So just relax and let the pretty nurses pamper you. And read the mystery novels we got for you."

He pointed to a stack of old paperbacks they'd brought from my house to keep me company.

"I suppose I got no choice," I said irritably.

"And everything did turn out good," Shamrock piped in.

"I guess so . . . except one thing."

"What's that?" Steve asked.

"Gant," I answered. "He saved my life, too."

Steve and Shamrock both had another good laugh over that. Then Steve said, "Don't worry about that, he would've pulled out a serial killer. He still doesn't like you."

I shook my head. "What could be worse than owing my life to Gant? Nothing that I can think of."

Just then there was a commotion out in the hallway. I heard a nurse's shrill voice. "You're not supposed to be out of your bed. Where do you think you're going?"

"Right down here," a male voice answered.

That voice, it was familiar. I couldn't place it at first, and then it dawned on me just as he came through the doorway and into my room—Eddie Hoar.

He had on nothing that I could see but a hospital johnny. His greasy black hair was a spiked-up mess from sleeping on it.

"Hi, everybody," he said, a silly grin plastered on his unshaven face.

Eddie turned, closed the door. I got a look at his scrawny, pale, pockmarked ass as he did. I was dumbfounded. I looked from Steve to Shamrock and back again.

Finally, Steve solved the puzzle. "We didn't have the heart to tell you. You got a neighbor."

"That's right, Dan," Eddie said cheerily as he walked over to my bed and stood beside Shamrock who was looking up at him and shaking his head. "You ain't going to be lonely. I'm in the room right down the hall. And I'm going to be here for a few days. They gotta run some tests. Somethin' about my kidneys. They said I almost died, too."

Shamrock harrumphed. "You would've, you arse, if you hadn't had a giant tolerance to all known drugs."

"That's not funny," Eddie said. "I'm a very sick man."

"Sick in the head," Shamrock said disgustedly.

I looked from one face to the other. Then it dawned on me, and my mood brightened a bit. "Oh, I get it. This is some kind of joke. That's it. You're all in on it. Eddie's not really a patient here."

Eddie still wore a stupid grin but Shamrock and Steve both looked a bit dejected.

"No joke," they both said almost in unison.

Eddie—right next door. For the next few days.

I wasn't sure I could take that.

I glanced at the window and wondered how many floors up we were. Whether to jump myself or toss Eddie out—I pondered both options.

"We got to get going," Steve said. "We both came in my car."

"Wait a second," I said desperately. "You're not going to leave me alone with . . ."

Shamrock and Steve both smiled as they got up and headed for the door, tossing their goodbyes over their shoulders.

"Wait . . ." I started but it was too late. They opened the door and closed it behind them.

I looked at Eddie. Instead of sitting on one of the vacant chairs, he plopped his bare ass down on the bed beside me and farted.

"Derwood'll be here most of the time to keep us company," Eddie said. "He doesn't know what to do without me."